PREGNANCY & BIRTH MADE CALM

THE EVIDENCE-BASED GUIDE FOR A SAFE, HEALTHY PREGNANCY AND A POSITIVE BIRTH EXPERIENCE

by

DR HARRIET FRASER

Medical Disclaimer

This book provides general information about pregnancy, birth, and related health topics, drawn from current medical evidence and clinical experience. It is intended for educational and informational purposes only.

It is not a substitute for personalised medical advice, diagnosis, or treatment. Every pregnancy and individual is different, and medical guidance should always be tailored to your specific circumstances.

If you have any concerns about your health, symptoms, or your pregnancy, consult your midwife, obstetrician, GP, or other qualified healthcare professional without delay. Never disregard professional medical advice or delay seeking it because of something you have read in this book.

While every effort has been made to ensure accuracy at the time of publication, medical knowledge and practice continue to evolve, and readers are encouraged to consult reputable sources and healthcare providers for the most current information.

DEDICATION

To my husband who was the best
birth partner I could wish for

and to

Rachel, Emily, Heidi, Jacqui, Jo, Megan and Rachael

Brought together on our profound
journey to motherhood.

Thank you for your support, friendship
and love over the years

ACKNOWLEDGEMENTS

Thanks to Greg for his unwavering support and to my children Will, Anna Rose and Elodie, who have taught me so much. Thanks to my sister Alice for her love, encouragement, and insights into Hypnobirthing, and to my friends Nicola, Gayle, Amanda, Kim, Lisa and Caroline, for their help, support and insights. Thank you also to my doula teacher Ana Paula, and to Ellen for the labor positions image.

Thank you to Rica of Rica Graphics for her inspired cover design and expert formatting.

PREGNANCY & BIRTH MADE CALM:

The Evidence-Based Guide for a Safe, Healthy Pregnancy and a Positive Birth Experience

CONTENTS

INTRODUCTION

As I prepared for the birth of my third child, I found myself in a new landscape and a new country—our family had relocated from London, England to Los Angeles, California. My first two births had been in London, both natural, both deeply formative experiences.

For my first, I gave birth squatting, gripping metal bars at a birthing center within a London teaching hospital. It felt instinctive, and most importantly, I was given the space to do it. The time of birth was recorded by Big Ben itself, visible through the large picture window of the room. And all of this was on the National Health Service (NHS)—free (at the point of delivery), comprehensive care for which I would never receive a bill.

With my second child, born at the same hospital, meconium was detected as my waters broke, which can be a sign of distress in the baby. This meant I had to move mid-labor from the birthing center to a nearby ward where the baby could be monitored. Gone was the picture-perfect view of the Houses of Parliament, but once again, with my husband's support, I was able to squat on the floor, and deliver my daughter naturally.

When I became pregnant with my third child in the United States, I wanted an experience as close as possible to my experience in the UK. I wanted to be delivered by those who were experts in natural birth, midwives. I found a group of midwives working at a major teaching hospital in Los Angeles. My prenatal care felt fairly comparable, though I had to travel into the hospital for every appointment instead of being seen at a local clinic. In the UK, prenatal care is managed almost entirely by your primary care team; hospital visits are reserved for complications, multiple pregnancies, or specialist needs. Most women are cared for by their local clinic team throughout pregnancy on the NHS , and then, when labor begins and they go to their local hospital, they are assigned a midwife to deliver their baby. There is no choosing a doctor as in the US system.

This difference underscores one of the most important truths about pregnancy and birth, and underpins all my thoughts, ideas and advocacy on this issue: **pregnancy is not a sickness. It is not a pathology. It is one of the most natural, physiological processes of life.** This book will emphasize that perspective throughout. What you need is the right support. In the UK, in a normal pregnancy, this work is carried out, overwhelmingly, by midwives, in hospitals, birth centers or homes. In the USA a small percentage of deliveries are solely carried out by midwives, in a home or birth center setting. In UK hospitals, Doctors are called if complications arise and medical intervention becomes necessary, particularly where instrumental deliveries or caesarean sections are needed, or there is a problem with the baby or mother. In the USA, the system generally dictates mothers choosing a doctor as their care provider.

I was a family doctor in the UK for many years. Doctors deal with pathology-the causes, mechanisms and effects of diseases, they are there when things go wrong with our health. Doctors largely like to do things. They like to prescribe and intervene. Remember this.

When it came time to deliver my third child, I met unexpected roadblocks. The focus was firmly on delivering in a bed. I hadn't anticipated this. How was gravity supposed to help me from a bed? I wanted another natural birth and knew, by this time, how to give myself the best chance of that. The bed was non-negotiable—a policy that still mystifies me. Fortunately, my midwife managed to attach a bar across the bed, allowing me to squat on the mattress. Not ideal, but better than lying flat. In that moment, what I needed most was my voice. The panic I felt when told I couldn't squat on the floor gave way to speaking up, finding a solution in that moment, and ultimately delivering my baby naturally.

Interestingly, just as I was delivering, a doctor appeared—having earlier popped her head in to offer an epidural. In many US hospitals, even if a Certified Nurse Midwife (CNM) is delivering the baby, they insist on an Obstetric Doctor being present at delivery for safety and liability reasons.

My interest in maternity care began long before my own pregnancies. I originally studied medicine at University College London, and as a 20-year-old medical student, I volunteered in a maternity hospital in Kathmandu, Nepal. That experience solidified my fascination with pregnancy and childbirth. I went on to complete family medicine training in Oxford and later worked as a family doctor in central London before moving to Los Angeles in 2008. Over the years, I have performed thousands of hours of prenatal care, delivered babies (in fact, I had to deliver ten natural births just to pass my obstetrics and gynecology unit as a student), and performed caesarean sections.

But beyond my professional training, I bring personal insights from my three natural births—spanning both the UK and the US. These experiences give me a unique perspective on how childbirth practices differ across these systems and cultures.

The purpose of this book is simple: **to empower you, especially if you are a first-time mother.** I want to provide you with smart, practical, and evidence-based advice so you can make informed choices and approach childbirth with confidence, not fear. Fear is something I noticed in expectant mothers immediately upon arriving in the US—fear seemed woven into conversations about pregnancy and birth. I am still not entirely sure why it is so prevalent. But pregnancy should not be rooted in fear. It should be a time of trust, confidence, and belief in your body.

You will receive advice from every corner—friends, family, social media, even strangers. Some stories may feel overwhelming or frightening. But with knowledge and preparation, you can filter out the noise and focus on what empowers you. Remember always: pregnancy and childbirth are natural, not an illness.

This book will begin with preparing for pregnancy and setting you up for success. From there, we will move through each trimester, exploring what is happening in your body and with your baby. We will cover labor and delivery in detail and touch on postpartum recovery and breastfeeding. Each chapter is designed to be practical, supportive, and clear, guiding you step by step.

The information you will find here is grounded in scientific research and medical expertise, combined with my personal experience. This is not just opinion—it is evidence-based advice you can trust.

I also recognize that every pregnancy is unique. This book is meant to be inclusive and adaptable, offering tools to help you make the choices that feel right for you and your family. Whether you are planning a hospital birth, a home birth, or something in between, my hope is that you feel supported and empowered throughout your journey from pregnancy to your new and profound role as a mother.

A few notes: This book is designed for readers that reflect my dual citizenship (UK and US) but I have generally used the American spelling of words. The equivalent of 'Healthcare Provider' in the US means your GP/Midwife/Obstetrician in the UK, depending on where you are in your journey and who is looking after you. There are pages in the back of the book for notes and birth plan ideas, so that as you read you can jot down thoughts that arise and things you may not want to forget to mention to your healthcare provider. There are many references to scientific research papers and other papers and guidelines in the back of the book, as well as general resources.

This concise book cannot, of course, cover the multitude of conditions that a number of people may have before embarking on pregnancy and all complications and conditions that arise during pregnancy and birth. It is also not a substitute for communicating with your Healthcare Provider. If something doesn't feel right or a new symptom is alarming, please don't wait. Trust your instincts and seek medical help.

PREPARING FOR PREGNANCY

Starting a family is one of life's most profound adventures. My husband and I had decided not to wait too long after getting married to embark on this journey as we were both in our thirties when we met. Navigating this new phase felt exciting yet daunting but we were secure in the knowledge that it was a journey we wanted to take. It's natural to wonder about the best steps to take, how to prepare, and what lies ahead. This chapter aims to guide you through those steps, providing a foundation grounded in knowledge and empowerment.

UNDERSTANDING YOUR BODY: PRECONCEPTION HEALTH ESSENTIALS

Your health is the cornerstone of a successful pregnancy. As you contemplate this first chapter, optimizing your health is a really good idea. It's not just about the physical aspects but also about mental readiness. The transition requires strength and resilience, both physically and mentally. Taking this time to focus on your lifestyle and habits is invaluable.

I'm well aware, as a doctor, that plenty of people get pregnant unexpectedly or without giving it much forethought, and you'll see how this happened to me a little later in the book! This is all part of the unpredictability of life. If you find yourself pregnant and you're reading this book, fantastic. You can skim this section or skip to Chapter 2. In fact, I didn't spend much time thinking about it beforehand. I knew I wanted to start a family and felt like my biological clock was ticking, and was honestly so busy with work that we simply started trying. Now writing this book and reflecting back, I felt it was important to start with preparation for those who are able to give the pre-pregnancy phase more time, thought and intention.

HEALTH CHECKS

Start by ensuring you're up to date with health checks. If you have any ongoing health concerns or pre-existing conditions, mental health conditions or a chronic illness, make an appointment with your healthcare provider. This is particularly important if you're taking medications that might need adjusting. Discussing your family medical history and considering genetic counseling can provide insights into any potential hereditary conditions. Don't overlook the importance of vaccinations and assessing your immunity status.

LIFESTYLE FACTORS

These also play a pivotal role in preconception health. If you **smoke**, I would strongly urge you to quit. Smoking will cause reduced oxygen delivery to your baby due to carbon monoxide and nicotine exposure, which can cause an increased heart rate in the baby and can cause reduced growth in the baby amongst other things.

Reduce **alcohol** consumption as much as possible, preferably to zero. There is no research to suggest that the odd glass of beer/wine/cocktail is harmful to your baby, but an amount that is safe has never been quantified and to keep the message clear, in both the US and UK, expectant mothers are told that no amount of alcohol is safe. The perils of large amounts of alcohol consumption and binge drinking in pregnancy are well-documented in the devastating condition 'fetal alcohol syndrome', which affects a baby's size, facial formation and brain development. The increasing popularity and ingenious new non-alcoholic alternatives to beer, wine and cocktails are well-worth exploring here.

Managing chronic conditions like diabetes or hypertension can significantly impact your pregnancy experience. Embrace a **balanced diet** rich in nutrients and make regular exercise part of your routine. These adjustments not only improve overall health but also increase the likelihood of a healthy pregnancy.

VITAMINS AND SUPPLEMENTS

Folic acid is essential for preventing neural tube defects like spina bifida, in your baby, so starting supplementation at least three months before conception is advisable. Spina bifida occurs when the neural tube (which develops into the brain and spinal cord early on in pregnancy) doesn't close completely. Take 400-600 mcg Vitamin D (at least 400 IU) to support bone health, while **iron** helps prevent anemia and supports fetal development. Some people find iron difficult to take, as it can cause gastrointestinal symptoms. I took an oral preparation which worked really well (for instance Floradix). Consult with your healthcare provider for personalized recommendations, but focus on maintaining a simple regimen that prioritizes a balanced diet and regular exercise.

MENSTRUAL CYCLE

Understanding your *menstrual cycle* is key to enhancing fertility awareness. The menstrual cycle consists of four phases: menstruation, the follicular phase, ovulation, and the luteal phase. Menstruation (your period), involves shedding the uterine lining and typically lasts 3 to 7 days. This marks the beginning of the cycle and it is a good idea to get into the habit of noting down the first day of your period. This becomes your LMP (last menstrual period) when you become pregnant and all dates will be calculated from this date. You will always be asked this when you become pregnant. The follicular phase begins after your period and involves the thickening of the uterine lining and growth of ovarian follicles. Ovulation occurs when a mature egg is released, usually about two weeks before your next period. The luteal phase follows ovulation, during which the egg travels through the fallopian tubes to the uterus. If fertilization doesn't occur, menstruation begins again.

Recognizing ovulation signs can help you identify your fertility window, increasing your chances of conception. Tracking your menstrual cycles can reveal patterns and provide insights into your body's rhythms. Some women notice physical changes like increased cervical mucus or basal body temperature fluctuations during ovulation.

To further support your understanding, consider keeping a journal or use an app to track your cycles. Note any patterns or symptoms you experience throughout each phase. This record can be invaluable when discussing fertility with your healthcare provider or making informed decisions about timing.

FERTILITY FUNDAMENTALS: OPTIMIZING YOUR CHANCES

It's really important to enter the pre-conception phase with positivity and excitement. Please, please at this point block out the tales of friends who took years to conceive; those stories can be heart-wrenching but thankfully they are not so common. Fertility reflects many factors, only some within your control. In my own journey, I conceived my first two relatively quickly (2-4 months) but when it came to conceiving my third child, we tried for two years and because we had two healthy children we had already decided not to embark on enhanced fertility measures, so we came to the conclusion it was not to be. I organised a yard sale and got rid of absolutely everything we might have needed for a newborn. Little did I know that at that very yard sale, I was already 2 weeks pregnant! It's not just a cliché, it was only when I stopped obsessing and worrying about getting pregnant, that it actually happened. Sometimes easier said than done but try not to obsess over it..

Age plays a crucial role in fertility. I conceived my third child when I was 42 and had her when I was 43. In your 20s and early 30s, your chances of getting pregnant are generally higher. As age advances, fertility naturally declines due to decreased egg quantity and quality. This isn't meant to alarm but to inform. Knowing this can help you plan realistically. Weight also affects fertility. Maintaining a healthy weight supports ovulation and reduces the risk of complications. Being underweight can disrupt hormonal balance, while being overweight may hinder ovulation.

Consider lifestyle tweaks to enhance fertility further. Eating antioxidant-rich foods like berries and nuts can improve reproductive health by combating oxidative stress. Reducing caffeine intake is beneficial too; excessive caffeine can affect fertility. Managing stress is equally pivotal. Techniques like yoga, breathwork and meditation can be transformative, lowering cortisol levels and promoting relaxation (more about this in Calm Birthing in Chapter 4).

Timing intercourse is another critical aspect. Understanding ovulation can maximize your chances of conception. Ovulation typically occurs midway through your cycle, generally 14 days before your next period starts. It is marked by a change in cervical mucus (it becomes more clear and stretchy) and/or a slight rise in basal body temperature (0.5-1 degree Fahrenheit). You can also experience ovulation pain (known as Mittelschmerz). Tracking these signs helps identify your fertility window. It's also important to know that sperm can remain alive in a woman's body for around 5 days, but an egg will only last 12-24 hours, so concentrate on engaging in intercourse BEFORE ovulation, at least in the 2-5 days leading up to ovulation, even on the day itself it is less effective, as the hormone progesterone is now increasing and it causes the mucus to become thicker again, which stops sperm moving so well.

You should be encouraged to hear that over all age groups, around 85% of couples will conceive naturally during the first year of trying, with regular intercourse. As I mentioned earlier, age is a big factor in fertility, so this percentage will be reduced in women over 35.

If natural attempts don't yield results within a year, you can consider assisted reproductive technologies (ART) if they are available to you. In vitro fertilization (IVF), intrauterine insemination (IUI) and Intracytoplasmic Sperm Injection (ICSI) offer alternative paths to parenthood. IVF involves fertilizing an egg outside the body before implanting it in the uterus, while IUI places sperm directly into the uterus during ovulation. ICSI is particularly used in male factor infertility where mature eggs are retrieved from the ovaries and a single healthy looking sperm is injected into the center of an egg, the fertilized egg then develops in the lab for a few days and then this growing embryo is placed into the uterus. These options provide hope for many couples facing fertility challenges. It's important to weigh factors like cost, emotional readiness, and potential success rates when exploring ART. IVF success rates vary but often range around 40% per cycle for women under 35.

ART isn't a one-size-fits-all solution. It's vital to consult with a reproductive specialist who can tailor treatments to your unique circumstances. Remember that ART may not be an immediate step unless other medical factors come into play; many couples successfully conceive within 1-2 years of trying naturally.

Navigating fertility can feel overwhelming, but knowledge empowers you to make informed decisions. Give yourself credit for any progress you make, whether it's through lifestyle changes, understanding your body's rhythms, or exploring new paths to parenthood. And try to use deep relaxation techniques (skip to Chapter 4 at any time for great breathing techniques) to aid a calm approach to fertility and getting pregnant.

FERTILITY CHECKLIST

- **Monitor Your Cycle:** Track signs of ovulation for better timing.
- **No smoking or recreational drugs** in you or your partner
- **Dietary Adjustments:** Incorporate antioxidant-rich foods and optimize weight.
- **Reduce Caffeine:** Limit intake for improved fertility.
- **Stress Management:** Practice breathwork, yoga or meditation.
- **Consult Specialists:** Consider ART if needed after a year.

NUTRITIONAL FOUNDATIONS: CREATING A PREGNANCY-FRIENDLY DIET

In this pre-conception period it's a great idea to review and ensure good nutrition. The focus should be on fostering an environment that supports not just your health and vitality, but also your growing baby. Earlier, I mentioned folate and folic acid playing an instrumental role in the prevention of neural tube defects, which are severe congenital malformations affecting the brain and spine of an unborn child. As well as supplementation with folic acid (the synthetic variant of folate) you can find sources in your diet. Folate can be readily found in an array of naturally occurring food sources such as leafy greens, lentils, and oranges.

EXPANDING ON PROTEIN AND DIET CHOICES

Protein constitutes another essential element in preconception nutritional health. It underpins the development and repair processes within tissue structures. Make sure your diet has a good amount of protein, and be especially careful to meet requirements in those with a specialty diet. It is useful to note that most people will easily meet their protein requirement with a normal healthy diet when not pregnant but it is good to eat more while pregnant, roughly 60g per day in the 1st trimester, then 70g in the second and 80g in the third, whereas when you're not pregnant 45g or so is a good amount. Explore options like lean meats, eggs, beans, and nuts—remember iron content in red meat can prevent anemia, while the fiber in beans aids digestive health. Beware of the explosion of the heavily processed 'protein bars' now on the market, and check for added ingredients including sugar content. My general rule of thumb with all foods is, if I can't pronounce an ingredient in the list given, it is probably quite processed and best avoided.

In your dietary planning, take care to avoid or eliminate certain items leading up to and during pregnancy. Fish varieties with high mercury content pose a risk to fertility and fetal development. Avoid consumption of species such as shark, swordfish, tile fish, king mackerel and, to a lesser extent, albacore tuna (skipjack tuna cans are ok), for this reason. Lean towards safer choices like salmon or sardines, which offer ample nutritional value without the associated risks of high mercury content.

With increasing evidence that ultra-processed foods cause harm, try to avoid processed foods as much as possible. These will contain unwelcome additives and can contain unhealthy fats (trans fats) that could impede fertility and general health. Trans fats, in particular, have been linked to heightened inflammation and insulin resistance. Prioritize whole foods wherever possible and check food labels!

These dietary modifications possess the potential to exert a profound and enduring influence on your fertility and pregnancy well-being, and, by focussing on it, may well help you develop sustained healthier habits, well after your baby is born.

NUTRITION CHECKLIST

- **Folate/Folic Acid:** Cook leafy greens for natural folate and add supplements for convenience and added assurance.
- **Omega-3s:** Enhance your diet with the inclusion of flaxseeds or salmon, sources rich in brain-boosting benefits.
- **Protein:** Broaden your protein horizons with an assortment of lean meats, eggs, and plant-based proteins like beans.
- **Limit High-Mercury Fish:** Opt for mercury-safe options like salmon over notorious high-mercury counterparts such as shark.
- **Avoid Trans Fats:** Favor whole foods and maintain vigilance with label-reading to steer clear of hidden trans fats.

VACCINES TO THINK ABOUT PRE-PREGNANCY

When thinking about vaccination pre-pregnancy/while pregnant and any potential harm to your unborn child, any vaccination that contains dead (not live) virus is deemed safe in pregnancy and each of these recommended vaccines has a specific reference cited in the back of the book if you want to read the evidence for safety. The medical terms used here are that **inactivated (non-live)** vaccines are safe but **live-attenuated** are not safe.

- **Influenza** ('flu) shot is a smart idea, and if you haven't had it before you are pregnant, it is safe to have during pregnancy. However, to be clear, the nasal spray flu vaccine 'FluMist' is NOT safe during pregnancy, this is a live attenuated vaccine to be avoided in pregnancy.

- **DTaP or diphtheria, tetanus and pertussis** (known as Adacel in the UK). There has been an increase in whooping cough (pertussis) in babies in the UK and US in recent years. Young babies can potentially get quite sick with this bacterial infection. It is suggested that even though you will likely have been immunized as a child, levels of immunity fall after several years, so it is recommended to get this booster. The antibodies you develop after the vaccine will be passed along to your baby, through the placenta, to protect them from whooping cough when they are very young. Research shows that if mothers have this booster vaccine during pregnancy their babies are 80% less likely to catch pertussis. You should have this booster sometime between 16 and 32 weeks.

- **COVID-19** mRNA vaccination is also safe and recommended before and during pregnancy. Again, antibodies you build up will be passed to your baby through the placenta. After pregnancy, even if you are breastfeeding, this vaccination is safe.
- Vaccinating mothers against **Respiratory Syncytial Virus (RSV)** around 32-36 weeks of the pregnancy will transfer protection against this potentially severe respiratory virus up to about 6 months of age. This vaccine is recommended but there is some evidence that it can increase preterm birth.

All these vaccines are offered in the US and UK to pregnant mothers. The World Health Organization particularly recommends Tdap and inactivated 'flu vaccine during pregnancy, worldwide. The Centers For Disease Control and Prevention (CDC) adds RSV and Covid-19 vaccinations to this list.

-vaccines to AVOID during pregnancy are those that contain live virus. Even if the virus is weakened (attenuated), they are not recommended during pregnancy. This includes the chicken pox vaccine and the measles, mumps and rubella vaccination known as MMR.

GENETIC SCREENING

Most people will carry a gene for a genetic disorder, even if it has never shown up in family history, but most disorders need the gene to be carried by both parents, so testing the father is only necessary if the mother tests positive or vice versa. Some genetic testing has historically been determined on geographical or ethnic background although this becomes harder to determine in today's multiethnic world. Advances in genetic screening in recent years now enable couples to test for multiple genetic conditions before conception, but there is debate about whether this should be offered in the mainstream. In the US they are more widely available. In the UK at this time, they are generally offered in specific circumstances where there is a family history of a particular genetic condition. If you have concerns about this, you should talk with your family doctor/OBGYN.

THE ROLE OF EXERCISE: PREPARING YOUR BODY FOR PREGNANCY

Embracing a regular exercise routine before pregnancy is a powerful step towards enhancing fertility and ensuring overall well-being. Exercise isn't just about physical fitness; it has profound effects on your cardiovascular health, mood, and stress levels. When you engage in consistent physical activity, your heart becomes more efficient at pumping blood, which benefits every part of your body, including your reproductive organs. A healthy heart supports better circulation, which can contribute to a more regular menstrual cycle and improved fertility. Beyond the physical, exercise can be a tremendous ally in boosting your mood and reducing stress. The endorphins released during a workout act as natural mood lifters, helping you tackle daily challenges with a positive mindset. This is especially beneficial when preparing for pregnancy, as stress can negatively impact fertility.

When considering exercise routines, it's important to focus on activities that you enjoy and that are safe for pre-pregnancy fitness. Low-impact exercises like walking and yoga are excellent choices. Walking is accessible to most people and can be done almost anywhere. It gently elevates your heart rate, improving cardiovascular health without putting undue strain on your body. Yoga, on the other hand, offers a blend of physical movement and mindfulness. It enhances flexibility, strengthens muscles, and promotes relaxation—key factors in preparing your body for the demands of pregnancy. Both activities can be easily adjusted to suit your fitness level and can be continued into pregnancy with appropriate modifications.

The frequency and duration of exercise should align with your personal comfort and schedule. Aim for at least 150 minutes of moderate aerobic activity each week, as recommended by health experts, which can be spread across several days, allowing you to integrate exercise into your routine without feeling overwhelmed. Listening to your body is crucial; it's perfectly okay to take rest days or mix up your activities to prevent burnout. Pay attention to how your body responds and adjust accordingly. It's a myth that exercise can harm fertility; in fact, regular physical activity supports hormonal balance and overall health.

Of course, while planning your exercise regimen, be mindful of any underlying health conditions or concerns and consult with your healthcare provider if you have questions or concerns.

There's a common misconception that intense workouts should be avoided when trying to conceive. While extreme training might not be advisable, maintaining a balanced routine of moderate intensity exercises is beneficial. The goal is to support your body's readiness for pregnancy without overexerting yourself.

Incorporating variety into your fitness routine keeps things interesting and engages different muscle groups. Consider adding swimming or cycling into the mix for a change of pace. These activities offer excellent cardiovascular benefits while being gentle on the joints, making them suitable for many women preparing for pregnancy, and indeed during pregnancy. I swam a lot while pregnant, not something I had been particularly prone to pre-pregnancy, but the feeling of weightlessness, especially in the later months, was worth every hassle of getting into that pool.

Think of the path to motherhood as a great opportunity to check in and connect with your body, understand its capabilities, appreciate its resilience and get to know it like never before. Regular physical activity will build a foundation of strength and endurance that will serve you well throughout pregnancy and beyond, and will nurture your body and mind.

EMOTIONAL READINESS: AVOIDING FEAR, STRESS, AND ANXIETY BEFORE CONCEPTION

The emotional landscape of preparing for pregnancy is vast and varied. It's easy to get caught up in the whirlwind of expectations and what-ifs. But before anything else, embrace positivity. I can't emphasize this enough! You do not want fear creeping in, anywhere on this journey, and certainly not before you are even pregnant. Try not to feel the pressure to meet certain timelines. Everyone's path to parenthood is different. More about this in Chapter 4 on Calm Birthing, but suffice to say, learn early on to block out the noise of negative stories around conception/pregnancy and birth. And I would even advise you to add in a simple breathing technique into your daily routine even now (again more about this in Chapter 4). A simple 4 count breath in through your nose and a slower 8 count outbreath through your mouth. Better still if this is something you haven't done before, then start with 4 in through your nose and 4 out through your mouth, then 4 in and 5 out, 4/6, 4/7 and build up to 4/8. It can help in many situations which make you fearful, worried or stressed, and can bring heightened emotions down. I even practice this in the break between games of a challenging tennis match. The point is you can do it literally anywhere. I have taught this to my children over the years. I was driving to an appointment with my 12 year old recently, I was anxious as we were running late. Mum, she said, do your breath. There is nothing we can do about the traffic! Even in the car, it can bring the anxiety/stress levels down. Try it any day, any time you can, even 5 breaths, I promise it will help you in any difficult situation and will certainly help you through the whole process of conception, pregnancy and childbirth. In fact, later it will be crucial. Practising it in your everyday life and training your body to step away from the fright/flight response that produces adrenaline, and into a calmer place, will be more useful than you know as we go through this journey. I will mention it regularly in this book. I'll call it the calm breath.

It's totally normal to feel apprehensive about what's to come but don't let these feelings overwhelm you or take away from the joy of planning a family. Are there unresolved issues or fears that could affect your experience or cause fear to creep in? Addressing them now can make a world of difference later on. Perhaps it's a fear of childbirth or even loss of pregnancy or fear of it, something many women experience but seldom discuss openly. Of course any kind of sexual trauma in your past can affect your thoughts profoundly. Sharing these delicate issues and concerns with a partner, friend, or therapist is very important and can be liberating.

Creating a supportive environment is key. Surround yourself with people who uplift and encourage you. Whether it's a partner, family, or friends, having a network you can lean on is invaluable. They will be there when doubt creeps in and will be a sounding board when you need to vent. And give yourself permission to seek help or support when things feel overwhelming. You're not alone in this! Building a community of people who are there to support and encourage now, will be invaluable all through this journey. More on that later.

Mindfulness practices like meditation and the calm breath we have already talked about, can be powerful tools in managing stress and anxiety. Also, journaling can be a useful tool through this journey. Writing down your thoughts and worries can provide clarity and insight. Don't forget the space for notes in the back of this book.

Routine activities can also serve as anchors during this period of preparation. Whether it's a morning walk, a favorite hobby, or simply enjoying a cup of tea in silence, these small rituals ground you in the present. They remind you that life is more than just planning for what's next.

It's important to remember that there's no perfect timeline for starting a family. Social media and societal pressures often paint an unrealistic picture of what it should look like. But real life doesn't follow a script. There's beauty in the unexpected and strength in adaptability. Trust that things will unfold as they should.

Chapter 1 Checklist:

HEALTH CHECKS & MEDICAL READINESS

- Schedule a preconception visit with your provider
- Review ongoing conditions, medications, and family history
- Update vaccines: flu, DTaP, COVID-19, RSV (if available)
- Avoid live vaccines (MMR, varicella) during pregnancy
- Consider genetic counseling if indicated

LIFESTYLE FOUNDATIONS

- Stop smoking and avoid recreational drugs
- Reduce alcohol to zero
- Limit caffeine (more in next chapter, but 1-2 cups is ok) and avoid trans fats/ultra-processed foods
- Maintain a healthy weight and manage chronic conditions
- Stay physically active

VITAMINS & NUTRITION

- Folic acid: 400–600 mcg daily (start ≥3 months before conception)
- Vitamin D: at least 400 IU daily
- Iron (dietary or supplements) to prevent anemia
- Balanced diet: lean protein, leafy greens, nuts, beans, omega-3s
- Avoid high-mercury fish (shark, swordfish, king mackerel, albacore tuna)

UNDERSTANDING YOUR CYCLE & FERTILITY

- Track your cycle and note your LMP (last menstrual period)
- Learn signs of ovulation: cervical mucus, temperature changes, mild pelvic pain
- Fertile window: starts 2–5 days before ovulation until 1 day after
- 85% of couples conceive within a year with regular intercourse
- Fertility declines gradually after mid-30s

FERTILITY SUPPORT

- Consider ART (IUI, IVF) if no pregnancy after 12 months (6 months if over 35)
- IVF success ~40% per cycle for women under 35

EXERCISE & PHYSICAL PREPARATION

- Aim for 150 minutes of moderate activity weekly
- Great options: walking, swimming, yoga, cycling
- Exercise improves fertility, mood, and cardiovascular health

EMOTIONAL READINESS

- Practice calm breath: inhale 4, exhale 6–8
- Journaling, mindfulness, and small rituals reduce stress
- Surround yourself with a supportive network
- Remember: pregnancy is natural, not a disease

NAVIGATING THE FIRST TRIMESTER (1-13 WEEKS)

Congratulations! Finding yourself pregnant can stir up a multitude of emotions. Some of you will be excited, especially if this is something you have been working towards. Many of you will feel an element of apprehension. Breathe and take it in, that calm breath we have already talked about. Use it whenever you need. You may well have mixed emotions, for so many reasons. I encourage you to use your supports and gradually ease into this new state. This is a life changing journey, but a natural process that your body was designed for. You are not sick and don't have a medical condition! You do not need to panic or be fearful. Gradually build out your support team from your immediate family to those who will be checking up on you along the way. This early phase, lasting up to 13 weeks, is crucial as your baby's organs begin to form, as you see in this FACTS FIRST section. It's a fascinating time of incredibly rapid changes and growth of your baby, and sometimes strange sensations.

Throughout pregnancy and this book, your 'hormones' or your 'pregnancy hormones' will be mentioned. Before we embark on this chapter and all the first trimester excitement and beyond, let me give you a quick run down of what that exactly means, and you can reference back to it when these are mentioned in the book.

YOUR HORMONES

Hormones are powerful messengers that orchestrate changes in nearly every system of your body. Pregnancy brings about extraordinary hormonal changes that guide your body through each stage. These hormones not only support your growing baby but also explain many of the physical and emotional changes you experience. They nurture your baby, prepare your body for birth, and then set the stage for bonding and feeding your newborn.

Human Chorionic Gonadotropin (hCG):
This is the hormone detected in pregnancy tests. Produced by the placenta soon after implantation, hCG signals your body to stop menstruation and supports early pregnancy. It peaks in the first trimester and often contributes to nausea and vomiting ("morning sickness").

Progesterone:

Levels rise steadily throughout pregnancy. Progesterone relaxes smooth muscle, which helps prevent early contractions, but it can also slow digestion, causing bloating or constipation. It plays a vital role in maintaining the uterine lining and supporting the placenta.

Estrogen/Oestrogen:

Estrogen production surges in pregnancy, stimulating blood flow to the uterus and placenta. It also helps the uterus grow and prepares breast tissue for milk production. High levels can contribute to mood swings and increased sensitivity.

Relaxin:

Appropriately named, relaxin loosens ligaments and joints to prepare the pelvis for birth. While essential for delivery, it can sometimes cause joint instability or back discomfort during pregnancy.

Oxytocin:

Known as the "love hormone", its release is triggered by physical touch such as hugging and cuddling and massage, emotional closeness and positive social interaction. It rises at the end of pregnancy and triggers uterine surges during labor. After birth, it helps the uterus shrink back to its pre-pregnancy size and promotes bonding and breastfeeding.

Prolactin:

This hormone is responsible for milk production. Levels increase during pregnancy but rise significantly after birth, helping establish breastfeeding.

Now let's get stuck into the first trimester.

FACTS FIRST

Definition of First Trimester: Week 1 to end of Week 13

Week 1: This is based on the LMP (the Last Menstrual Period, ie the first day of your last period that I mentioned before). It's a date we can pinpoint, unlike when the sperm and egg actually meet, so it's called week 1 even though you're not actually pregnant yet!

Week 2: The lining of the uterus is thickening to prepare for a fertilized egg. Towards the end of this week, ovulation will occur (where follicles in your ovary are maturing and one becomes dominant and then releases an egg).

- **FUN FACT** This is the week I had my yard sale 3rd time round!

Week 3: The egg will start to travel along the fallopian tube where, if conditions are right and sperm are present, it will meet sperm and that fertilized egg will travel on to your uterus. It's this week that you have actually conceived and are pregnant! Congratulations!

Week 4: Implantation occurs! The fertilized cells (within hours of sperm meeting egg) continue to divide rapidly, and can now be called an embryo. This settles into the lining of the uterus. Half of the cells become the placenta which connects your baby to the mother, and the other half is your growing baby. The amniotic sac develops which is the bag of fluid around the baby.

Week 5: Your embryo is about the size of an orange seed. The heart is forming and will start beating.

Week 6: Baby's heart is now going at about 110 beats per minute, and is the size of a pea. The cheeks, jaw, ears, eyes, kidneys, liver and lungs are all developing.

Week 7: Baby is the size of a blueberry!! New brain cells are developing as are the legs, arms, mouth and tongue.

Week 8: Baby is now at the raspberry-sized stage of growth! Looking more baby-like than the tadpole-type shape of week 5 or so. The heart is now beating even quicker at 150-170 bpm and your baby is starting to make little movements.

Week 9: Your baby is now the size of an olive. Muscles are forming and the head is growing.

Week 10: Baby is at prune size. Cartilage and bones are forming as well as teeth under the gums. The stomach is producing digestive juices and the kidneys are already working to produce urine, and the boy baby testes or balls are producing the hormone testosterone.

Week 11: I like to think of this week as brussels sprout size. Love brussels sprouts. Hair and nails are developing and the body is straightening out more. Ovaries are forming in girl babies.

Week 12: Baby is now the size of a lime, growth is quite astonishingly rapid! All systems are formed but still developing.

Week 13: This marks the end of your first trimester, at the end of week 13, counting from the FIRST DAY OF YOUR LAST PERIOD (LMP). Baby is at lemon size and the head is half the size of the full length. The body will grow more as time goes on so the proportions will change.

As you can see, during this time, your body is working tirelessly, and you can understand why it might be leaving you a little bit drained. It is exhausting just reading about the changes taking place above, let alone the changes to your body! The placenta, a remarkable organ, begins to develop, attached to your uterine wall, acting as a lifeline between you and your baby. It provides nutrients and oxygen while removing waste. It's fascinating to think of the formation of this vital element of pregnancy, setting up the support system your baby needs. This intricate process can leave you feeling more fatigued than usual, as your body prioritizes supporting this new life over your usual energy levels.

The first trimester is often a rollercoaster of symptoms. You may notice changes like nausea, commonly known as morning sickness, although it can strike at any time of day. Hormonal shifts, particularly the rise in hCG (human chorionic gonadotrophin) levels, play a significant role in these feelings. It's not just about nausea; these hormones contribute to breast tenderness and the frequent need to urinate. We will be discussing management of many of these symptoms a little later in this chapter.

Partners can be an important source of support from the very beginning of this journey. Encourage them to engage by preparing meals or snacks and offering emotional reassurance when you're feeling overwhelmed. Open conversations about what you're experiencing can foster understanding and strengthen your bond. Sharing this journey together can make it all the more meaningful. And these feelings and sensations won't last your whole pregnancy. It is these initial weeks, with possible nausea/

vomiting and exhaustion, that can be some of the most trying.

As you settle into this new chapter, remember that it's normal to feel a mix of emotions. Hormones can affect your mood, leaving you exhilarated one moment and tearful the next. Lean into these feelings as part of the process and write down your thoughts if it helps. Don't forget that calming 4/8 breath. Use it at any time, a few quiet minutes, even in your car when you arrive somewhere, before you step out. Even 4-8 breaths can settle or calm you in an anxious moment.

IN THIS CHAPTER WE WILL DISCUSS:

- Early signs of pregnancy
- Choosing your HCP
- Morning sickness
- Fatigue
- Other symptoms of early pregnancy
- Nutrition
- Understanding your prenatal appointments
- Genetic testing
- Emotional Changes

A quick note: as you move through this trimester, and subsequent ones, don't forget to write down any thoughts or worries week to week in the notes section at the back. That way, it will remind you to mention to your provider at your next visit if the symptom doesn't subside. Many of these symptoms are all part of the body preparing for birth and growing your baby.

EARLY SIGNS OF PREGNANCY: WHAT TO EXPECT AND WHEN TO TEST

Finding out you're pregnant can be both thrilling and daunting. This usually comes with a missed period. If your cycle is usually regular, this absence can be a significant clue. But it's not the only sign. You might notice your breasts feeling tender or swollen, a change that many women experience due to hormonal shifts. You might also find yourself making more trips to the bathroom, as increased urination becomes part of your daily routine. This happens because your body is adjusting to the extra blood volume, leading your kidneys to work overtime.

When it comes to confirming your suspicions, timing is key. For the most accurate results, it's best to wait until **after your missed period** to take a pregnancy test (which means you would be roughly 4 weeks pregnant, taken as always, from the LMP). Testing too early might give you a false negative (meaning negative when you are actually pregnant), and looking back on the early weeks in FACTS FIRST confirms why this is. Follow the test instructions carefully, as each brand might have different guidelines. A morning test can be more accurate because your hCG levels are concentrated in the first urine of the day. If you're unsure, don't hesitate to repeat the test in a few days or consult a healthcare provider for a blood test, which can detect pregnancy sooner. The test measures hCG, which is a hormone produced by the placenta.

Once you've seen that positive result you can schedule your first prenatal appointment. Make sure you are taking FOLIC ACID or start now (mentioned in Chapter 1, to reduce the risk of neural tube defects). No big hurry for the first appointment but a good idea to see your provider/ GP/Midwife by 8-10 weeks so best to schedule right away in case there is a wait. This initial visit typically involves confirming your pregnancy and discussing your medical history.

It is important to know you're not alone in this adventure. Of course you will share the joy with your partner and maybe a trusted friend or family member initially, if you're comfortable doing so. You may want to leave the bigger announcement until 8-10 weeks as everything gets established, but it is very personal-do what feels right for you. Building community right from the get go is essential for the support you will need through this process and when you are finally a mother. Support can be invaluable as you navigate the physical and emotional changes ahead. Embrace the excitement but also acknowledge any apprehensions you might feel—it's all part of the experience.

While your body begins its transformation, take moments to connect with this new reality. Journaling can be a therapeutic way to document your thoughts and feelings. Consider setting goals for self-care and nurturing routines that prioritize rest and nourishment. This time is about honoring both your needs and those of the growing life within you. And remember your body is designed for this remarkable process.

CHOOSING THE RIGHT HEALTHCARE PROVIDER: WHAT TO CONSIDER

Here the UK and the USA differ quite substantially but I'd like to reflect on this for a minute before moving on.

For sure it would be ideal to have a comfortable, trusting relationship with your provider which can help to keep your pregnancy experience calm and without fear.

In the USA, many people have the luxury of selecting a healthcare provider. It is often a doctor but can be a midwife depending on your wants and needs and delivery destination. In the UK, you might see a mix of your family doctor (who you would likely know and trust), and a midwife that covers the geographical area of your doctor's office. This community midwife is a specialist in pregnancy and natural birth. In the UK, they will then visit you after you get home from the hospital, and cover any particular postpartum needs for the first 10 days of your baby's life, including support with breastfeeding. Always remember that pregnancy is a natural, physiological process, not an illness, and in many cultures doctors are not generally involved unless there are complications needing delivery assistance or surgery.

The most important thing is that you want your provider, whether that be a doctor or midwife, to be someone you can communicate with openly and who respects your preferences and concerns.

My first two children were born in London. Of course, being a doctor, I was at an advantage in knowing what they would be doing-checking the baby was growing appropriately by measuring fundal height (more on this later), listening to the baby's heart, checking for any blood tests that might need doing, checking my urine, blood pressure and overall wellbeing and preparing for the baby's arrival and discussions about my birth ideas/plans and what I would do when labour started.

The point is it was all quite straightforward and I knew my family/primary care doctor. When you become pregnant in the UK you continue seeing your doctor and their team at the office you know. You don't need to find another doctor. Because it is a normal part of life the carte is seamless in this way. I had routine pregnancies. It's routine for the vast majority of mothers to be. Of course, problems can arise which may need further intervention or investigation, and then supervision by an Obstetric doctor would be necessary, in UK.

In the US, you need to find a doctor or midwife who can look after you during your pregnancy. I will call that person your HCP (your health care provider) from now on. If you want to have a natural delivery in the USA, I would make sure to ask how many natural deliveries the doctor (OBGYN) had completed, or maybe, consider finding a Certified Nurse Midwife (CNM) to take care of you, a specialist in natural deliveries, if that is what you want, or a hospital that has CNM's as providers. They almost always work with a doctor (OBGYN) who they would consult if there were any problems along the way or during delivery. I knew when I was pregnant with my third and finding myself in more unfamiliar territory (in the USA), and wanting a 3rd natural delivery, that I was very pleased to find what I considered to be the closest thing to the antenatal/prenatal care I received in the UK. I found the midwife group at UCLA, and they saw me right through the pregnancy. My husband was sure that he wanted me to be in a hospital for the delivery, and I was ok with that, everyone has their preferences and comfort level, and we knew then that more extensive medical care or interventions would kick in immediately if there were any issues.

Again, In the USA, make sure your potential provider is understanding of your wishes and that you are being heard. What is their approach to pregnancy and childbirth? Are they supportive of the birth plan you envision? We will talk about this plan in detail in Chapter 5. Some providers may have specific protocols or preferences that might influence your choices. For example, if you're considering a vaginal birth after cesarean (VBAC), ensure your provider supports it and has experience with such deliveries. A friend of mine, also on her 3rd pregnancy (with twins) asked 10 doctors before she found one that would deliver her twins naturally.

Consider logistical aspects too. Location and availability matter more than you might think. The convenience of visiting your provider can ease stress during this period. Check their office hours, proximity to your home or workplace, and the ease of scheduling appointments. These practical details can significantly affect your overall experience.

In the UK, all your care will be free at the point of delivery (as part of the NHS or National Health Service), unless you opt to 'go private'. There are certainly plenty of private doctors and midwife groups in the UK and some employers will pay for their employees to be on a private health plan but the vast majority of women in the UK give birth in the NHS system so no money changes hands, it is paid for through your taxes, and national insurance contributions that come from your wages. On the NHS, women are seen by their primary care team prenatally and delivered by a midwife, at home, in a birth center or in a hospital, unless complications arise.

In the USA however, the situation is entirely different. The vast majority of people (92% in 2023) have some kind of health insurance plan whether private (65% or public 35%). Your health insurance plan will play a crucial role in your decision on a healthcare provider. You need to verify that the provider is within your network to avoid unexpected expenses and what your insurance covers regarding prenatal visits, tests, and hospital fees to give you peace of mind as you plan financially for a new addition to the family.

Recommendations can be incredibly valuable. Speak with friends or family who have had positive experiences with their providers. But also understand that some insurance plans will not cover just any provider, that you may have less choice if you don't want any out of pocket expenses. You can also look at online reviews and forums but I would caution reading too much on the internet as you may come across unhelpful stories that we talked about earlier that can upset the calm. Take care, there is almost too much choice and it can feel overwhelming!

Above all, trust your instincts. If something feels off during an initial consultation, don't hesitate to explore other options. You want to feel comfortable and supported throughout your pregnancy. And you want people around you who are comfortable and experienced with natural birth. This is a natural physiological process, always remember that!

We will now talk about some of the symptoms and sensations you might experience early on in your pregnancy.

COPING WITH MORNING SICKNESS: STRATEGIES FOR RELIEF

Morning sickness, despite its misleading name, can strike at any hour. It's one of those pregnancy quirks that's both a rite of passage and a challenge. Hormonal changes, particularly the rise in hCG levels, are the culprits here. They're working hard to support your baby's development but often leave you feeling queasy. But not always. Don't think there is anything wrong if you do not experience this symptom, you are one of the lucky ones. For some, it's a mild inconvenience; for others, it's a daily battle that can be debilitating. Understanding this process doesn't make it any less frustrating, but knowing that it's a sign of a healthy pregnancy might offer some solace.

Finding relief is personal, and what works for one person might not work for another. Eating small, frequent meals can also help maintain blood sugar levels and keep nausea at bay. The idea is to avoid an empty stomach, which can exacerbate feelings of sickness. Ginger is a popular remedy; sipping ginger tea or taking ginger supplements can ease nausea. These options are natural and gentle on the stomach. Acupressure wristbands, often used for motion sickness, apply pressure to specific points on your wrist and can offer relief for some. They're worth a try if you're searching for non-medical options.

Knowing when to seek medical advice is crucial. If you're experiencing severe dehydration or significant weight loss due to an inability to keep food down, it may be more than just morning sickness. Conditions like hyperemesis gravidarum, a severe form of morning sickness, require medical attention to prevent complications. It's important to trust your instincts and consult your healthcare provider if you're concerned about your symptoms. They can provide guidance and treatment options to help you manage your condition effectively.

Partner support during this time is essential. Simple gestures like preparing meals or snacks can ease the burden. Encouraging words and practical help can go a long way in making you feel supported.

Morning sickness is often portrayed as just another quirky part of pregnancy, but for many, it's a real struggle that impacts daily life, and your routines. While it can be disheartening to deal with constant nausea, remember that this phase is almost always temporary. Focusing on getting through each day and seeking support when needed, can help you navigate this challenging time. Each day is one step closer to the next stage where these feelings are likely to have passed. For the vast majority of women, me included, I felt much better after this first trimester. You can do this!

MANAGING FATIGUE: ENERGY-BOOSTING TIPS FOR MOTHERS-TO-BE

The first trimester often brings waves of fatigue that can hit you like a ton of bricks. It's not just you; there's a biological reason behind it. As your body adapts to the increased levels of progesterone, a hormone crucial for maintaining pregnancy, you'll start feeling more tired than usual. Progesterone helps relax the muscles in your body, which supports the expansion of your uterus. However, this relaxation can also slow down your metabolism, leading to that pervasive tiredness. Moreover, the energy demands of developing your baby are significant. Your body is working overtime to support the early stages of fetal development, diverting energy from your usual activities to focus on growing a new life. It's like your body has taken on a new, full-time job.

To combat this fatigue, consider incorporating short naps into your day. Even a quick 20-minute rest can do wonders to recharge your energy levels. Staying hydrated is another simple yet effective strategy. Dehydration can exacerbate fatigue, so keep a water bottle nearby and sip throughout the day. Water helps transport nutrients to your cells and flushes out toxins, supporting overall energy levels and well-being.

Making lifestyle adjustments can make a significant difference in how you manage fatigue. Establishing a consistent sleep schedule helps regulate your body's internal clock, making it easier to fall asleep and wake up refreshed. Aim for at least seven to eight hours of sleep each night. Additionally, incorporating light exercise like walking can enhance energy levels by boosting circulation and releasing endorphins, those feel-good hormones that lift your mood. Exercise doesn't have to be intense or lengthy; even a short stroll around the block can invigorate you and shake off some of that sluggishness.

Self-care during this time isn't just a luxury; it's a necessity. Setting realistic goals and managing expectations can prevent overwhelm and allow you to focus on what truly matters. Don't hesitate to delegate tasks when possible or ask for help if you need it. Practicing relaxation techniques like the breathing technique I have mentioned (the 4/8 breath) or even a guided meditation. You can use apps on your phone with good guided meditations, some specifically pregnancy related. At the time of going to press, I would recommend Headspace, Calm and Insight Timer, which all work in the US/UK. These can also help to reduce stress and improve your energy levels. These practices help center your mind and body, and they are laying the groundwork for techniques that will prove valuable all through your pregnancy and most crucially for your labor and birthing your baby.

And......

Honestly, every mother is different, but apart from the nausea and exhaustion, here's a quick guide to other symptoms you may experience in these first 3 months. These are all normal. And you may have all of these or none or somewhere in between, everyone is different. You can write notes in the back of the book on sensations and symptoms you experience, to discuss with your provider.

YOUR BODY IN THE FIRST TRIMESTER

More saliva production: you can find pooling of saliva in your mouth during this first trimester, harmless but annoying! It will likely disappear after the first few months. Top tip: chewing gum, brushing your teeth regularly or using a minty mouthwash.

More frequent urination: again your hormones will cause increased blood flow (fun fact: as your pregnancy progresses, your blood volume will nearly double during your pregnancy, (starting at about 10 weeks), and with this you also see increased urine flow. The kidneys also become more efficient at getting rid of waste, AND you will be getting rid of waste from your growing baby too. I'm afraid this is one of the symptoms that will not miraculously disappear in your second trimester. As your baby grows, your uterus will press on your bladder, leaving less space for urine. Don't fight it! You still need to stay hydrated, keep drinking plenty of water, and cut down on caffeine which can increase urination also.

A change in vaginal secretions: these can increase in the first trimester, again related to hormonal changes causing increased blood flow. It is generally thin and milky white, and does not tend to smell.

A metallic taste in your mouth: As with most symptoms during this time, it's related to a drastic change in your hormones, but as they settle, this symptom should disappear again within a few months. Use acid based substances to counteract it, like citrus fruit, or rinsing your mouth with salt water.

Breast tenderness/changes: Again your hormonal changes will cause your breasts to grow. Also you may notice the areola, the darker area around the nipple, may darken. You may also see more prominent veins on your breasts. Tenderness along with this growth usually subsides by the 3rd or 4th month.

Food cravings/aversions/appetite changes: this will be very individual but all or none of these symptoms can occur in pregnancy.

Lightheadedness/dizziness: this is also related to the hormonal changes in blood flow and the heart working harder.

Aching or pressure in lower abdomen: it is common to experience a cramping feeling or at least pressure in your lower abdomen, as blood flow increases and your uterus starts to grow.

Constipation: this can be common early on. Make sure to increase your fiber intake and drink plenty of water.

A rounding of your abdomen: this will become more obvious later in this first trimester and your clothes may start to feel more snug.

Some women can experience some **spotting** in the first trimester, which means that you notice some blood on the tissue when you wipe in the bathroom. This can, of course, be a very scary phenomenon. In fact 1 in 4 women may experience some bleeding in early pregnancy and most go on to have healthy pregnancies. This can occur when the embryo implants in the uterus. It can also occur if you have a pap smear during pregnancy or can occur after sex- the cervix at the top of your vagina is an area where the blood vessels are engorged or swollen during pregnancy and can be irritated in those circumstances. Occasionally a subchorionic bleed can occur where blood has collected, usually between the embryo and the placenta. These tend to resolve on their own, but certainly cause an inordinate amount of stress. You can call your provider for advice in these situations and they will decide if further investigations are necessary.

POSSIBLE PREGNANCY-RELATED REASONS TO CALL YOUR PROVIDER RIGHT AWAY INCLUDE:

- **Vaginal bleeding**

- **Severe abdominal pain**

- **Shoulder tip pain** (this can occur in ectopic pregnancy where the fetus is growing outside the uterus, usually in the fallopian tube, this is a medical emergency). This is usually accompanied by abdominal pain and often vaginal bleeding or spotting

- **Sudden/excessive thirst and reduced need for urination**

- **Painful urination accompanied by fever**

- **Visual disturbance**

- **Sudden/severe swelling of hands, face**

- **Severe headache that doesn't go away**

- **Difficulty breathing**

- **Severe vomiting**

- **Later in pregnancy, from third trimester, if you feel reduced fetal movements** (from 28 weeks on, you should be able to count 10 movements in 2 hours)

This list is not complete as there can be unexpected symptoms which may relate to pregnancy, or not. The rule of thumb is, if you are feeling unwell and worried then call your healthcare provider.

FIRST TRIMESTER NUTRITION: WHAT YOU NEED AND WHAT TO AVOID

First things first. You are going to gain weight, there is no way around that. You're not just eating for yourself anymore; you're nourishing the tiny life inside you, every moment of every day, thanks to the amazing placenta. This organ is your baby's lifeline, supplying oxygen and nutrients while removing waste. Essentially, it acts as the intermediary between you and your baby, ensuring everything they need gets through. So, while it might feel like you're constantly snacking, remember it's for a good cause.

Try not to fixate on the numbers on the scale. Maybe try not to weigh yourself at all. Instead, focus on eating intuitively. Your body will tell you what it needs—sometimes that's a salad, other times it might be a chocolate bar. When I was pregnant with my second, my cravings leaned heavily toward candy. It's okay to indulge occasionally, but having some healthy snacks like nuts or fruit around can help balance those cravings when hunger strikes unexpectedly.

Trust me, those moments will pop up more often than you think!

You'll notice that you're not just gaining weight in one place. This weight comes from various sources: the baby, the placenta, amniotic fluid, increased breast tissue, a higher blood volume, extra fluid retention, and even fat stores. All of these add up, and before you know it, you might gain over 30 pounds. And that's perfectly normal! Your body is doing an incredible job of creating a safe environment for your baby.

When it comes to what to eat, focus on whole foods that give you energy and nourishment. Think leafy greens, lean proteins, whole grains, and plenty of fruits and veggies. These foods provide essential vitamins and minerals needed for both you and your developing baby. But be aware of what to avoid too. Seafood high in mercury, like swordfish and king mackerel, is best to steer clear of. Caffeine is another one to monitor—try limiting your intake to keep within safe levels for pregnancy. In both the US and UK, recommendations state keeping caffeine intake at less than 200mg/day, which is the equivalent to 1-2 coffees depending on type/size of coffee, but remember the caffeine in some sodas and energy drinks and make sure you don't exceed the maximum recommended. Studies involving much higher caffeine levels suggest an effect on fetal growth, miscarriage and preterm birth.

You do not need to make drastic changes to your diet but being intuitive, mindful of avoiding the more processed foods, and having healthier snacks on hand for those hungry moments will be very helpful.

With food in pregnancy my usual mantra is eat well and eat often!

If you're reaching for supplements, make sure they're tailored to pregnancy needs. Prenatal vitamins can be helpful, ensuring you get enough folic acid and iron. These nutrients are vital for preventing neural tube defects and supporting your increased blood volume. It's always a good idea to chat with your healthcare provider about any supplements to ensure you're on the right track. Many women are deficient in Vitamin D so it's worth making sure your prenatal vitamins include vitamin D. Be careful with some of the prenatal supplements marketed out there, it's a wild world navigating the supplement business! Make sure you're getting folic acid, iron if your doctor thinks you need it from blood test results (and this is usually not until at least half way into the pregnancy), and vitamin D. Some supplements can cause significant abdominal symptoms so take care not to overload your system with unnecessary ones.

Beyond nutrition, hydration plays a crucial role in maintaining your health during this trimester. Your body is using more fluids than usual, due to this huge increase in blood volume and flow I have mentioned, so drinking enough water is key. It helps with digestion, keeps you energized, and can even alleviate some nausea symptoms.

UNDERSTANDING PRENATAL APPOINTMENTS: YOUR FIRST DOCTOR VISIT

We've already talked about healthcare providers in pregnancy and the differences between the UK and the USA.

I will keep reminding you of this as it is an important concept that can get lost in certain systems: pregnancy isn't a medical condition—it's an incredible and normal part of life.

In the end, your healthcare provider, wherever you are in the world, is there to support your choices and provide expert guidance. One that respects your wishes and ensures both you and your baby are healthy and happy through these transformative months.

Your first appointment will likely include, but can vary:

- confirming pregnancy if necessary
- a complete medical history
- physical exam (likely to include a baseline weight. You should not require a vaginal examination at this point, so you can always decline that if it is

mentioned.) NB if you are due for a Pap smear that can and may be done at this appointment, and will not harm the baby, although can cause slight spotting.

- urine test- a dip of your urine to check for sugar (glucose), blood, bacteria
- blood test for Rh (Rhesus) status, (see below for explanation)
- antibody levels for immunity to diseases such as rubella (german measles) NB: as previously mentioned it is important to make sure you are up to date with german measles (rubella) vaccination as this cannot be given during pregnancy and if a mother contracts this illness during pregnancy, it can be passed easily to the baby possibly causing miscarriage, stillbirth or significant fetal abnormalities.
- possibly genetic tests depending on family history, also possibly a blood sugar test if you have had gestational diabetes before, or a family history of diabetes

Rhesus: not to over complicate things but cells in the body have 'antigens' on them which can trigger an immune response causing antibodies to be produced. The red blood cells in the body usually have an antigen on their surface called the Rhesus factor (making people Rh or Rhesus positive) but some people lack it (Rh negative).

This is of no consequence, unless you are pregnant. If a Rh negative Mum is carrying a Rh positive baby (having inherited the Rh factor from the Rh positive Dad), the mother's red blood cells don't 'match' the baby's so if any of those Rh positive fetal blood cells were to enter the Rh-negative mothers circulation (they can sometimes cross the placenta) her immune system will make antibodies to them (because the Mum's body would see them as foreign). These don't generally matter for the first pregnancy but if there are enough antibodies built up during the first pregnancy then the second time around they can then attack the baby's blood cells causing potentially serious anemia (lack of red blood cells). This is known as Rhesus incompatibility. It is usually treated with the Rh negative pregnant mother being given an injection of Rh-immune globulin RhoGAM at around 28 weeks of pregnancy. This gives the mother antibodies to remove any Rh-positive cells before the mothers immune system notices them- to stop Mum from making antibodies. If blood tests show that the baby is Rh positive then another injection is given to the Mum about 3 days after birth. This injection needs to be given also if any invasive procedures take place during the pregnancy or if there is vaginal bleeding, and also if there is a miscarriage or ectopic pregnancy in the first pregnancy, to prevent problems in any subsequent pregnancy.

GENETIC TESTING DECISIONS IN THE FIRST TRIMESTER

This needs to be discussed with your partner and your healthcare provider. There are a number of options. You both will need to discuss the implications of having tests and a possible positive result and any action you might take. Don't go into these blindly, make sure to have the important and sometimes difficult conversations before you test.

SCREENING TESTS

Before we delve into screening tests, I want to be clear. You and your partner can decide from the very outset what kind of screening you want and whether you even want it at all. Screening tests will give you a likelihood that your baby may or may not have a condition or genetic abnormality. If needed you can proceed with diagnostic testing (see below). If you are sure that you would continue with a pregnancy whatever the results of testing, then screening tests, and certainly diagnostic tests, will possibly cause a pregnancy full of anxiety, and with diagnostic tests, even the loss of the baby. You can discuss this with your provider, who should make it clear that you have a choice in this matter. A friend of mine was made to feel like a terrible mother to be for deselecting screening blood tests. This is absolutely your choice, and I would hope no-one will judge you for it. It is exquisitely personal to each family and their beliefs, history and ideas.

Carrier screening: this will often depend on family history. Diseases such as thalassemia, sickle cell (both blood disorders), cystic fibrosis and Tay-Sachs can be screened for with blood or saliva testing.

First-trimester screening: done between 10 and 13 weeks, this includes blood test and nuchal fold thickness ultrasound scan, which is a measure of space at the baby's neck, where fluid can collect in certain chromosomal abnormalities. This tests for Down's Syndrome (or Trisomy 21), trisomy 18 and neural tube defects.

Cell-free fetal testing: Again this can be done at 10-13 weeks, also known as noninvasive prenatal testing. This checks for chromosomal abnormalities 13, 18 and 21, and can check on the baby's sex and the sex chromosomes.

DIAGNOSTIC TESTS

These can be done if any screening tests (above) show a high risk for a certain genetic problem. They will give an actual diagnosis.

Amniocentesis: done between 15 and 20 weeks of pregnancy. A needle is inserted into the mother's abdomen to collect some amniotic fluid which surrounds the baby. Risk of loss 0.5-1%, which is above background miscarriage risk.

Chorionic Villus Sampling (CVS): this test takes a sample from the early placenta and can be done earlier than amniocentesis, at 10 to 13 weeks. Risk of loss is 1-2% which is above background miscarriage risk.

To end this chapter, I want to emphasize and discuss the emotional impact of these early weeks of this momentous journey.

EMOTIONAL CHANGES: NAVIGATING THE ROLLERCOASTER

The emotional ride of early pregnancy can feel like a whirlwind. Hormones are the primary drivers here, causing your mood to swing like a pendulum. One moment, you're filled with excitement imagining the tiny life growing within you; the next, anxiety creeps in, whispering all sorts of worries. It's these hormonal shifts that make you feel like you're on an emotional rollercoaster, amplifying feelings you might have easily brushed off before. You're not alone in this; many women experience similar fluctuations, and it's perfectly normal.

Managing these highs and lows requires a bit of strategy. Mindfulness practices can offer a sense of calm amidst the storm. By focusing on your breath and being present in the moment, you create a space where anxiety has less room to grow. Journaling is another powerful tool. Remember to use the 4/8 breath tool as often as you need.

Open communication with loved ones can make a huge difference. Sharing your feelings with your partner, family, or friends not only lightens your emotional load but also strengthens your support network. They can offer comfort and reassurance, helping to steady you when things feel overwhelming. Building this network is essential: it catches you when those emotional dips feel steep. Don't be afraid to reach out and ask for help—people want to support you but don't always know how.

Sometimes, though, these emotional changes may need more than just a chat with a friend. If you find that feelings of sadness or anxiety persist, it might be time to seek professional help. Recognizing signs of prenatal depression or anxiety is crucial. You might notice changes in sleep patterns, appetite, or an inability to find joy in things you once loved. These are signals that warrant attention from a mental health professional and there are resources available.

I want to also mention at this point that some early pregnancy will end in miscarriage, which has nothing to do with your pre-pregnancy preparation or anything you do in early pregnancy. It is a fact of life and can take a large emotional toll which should not be underestimated. It can be as high as 15-20% in very early pregnancy, and gradually goes down, so that by the time you get to 2 months it is around 5% and decreases from there. Please, if this happens to you, I urge you to seek help and support from your partner, family and friends, and possibly a therapist who specialises in pregnancy loss.

As we wrap up this chapter, remember that these emotional changes, while challenging, are part of the incredible transformation happening within you. They connect deeply to the bigger picture of pregnancy—a time of growth and adaptation, both for you and your baby. By understanding and managing these emotions, you're setting the foundation for a healthy pregnancy experience. Next, we'll explore the second trimester, often known as the "honeymoon period" of pregnancy, where many find relief from early symptoms and energy is renewed.

Chapter 2 Checklist:

EMOTIONS AND MINDSET

- Finding out you're pregnant can bring a mix of joy, disbelief, excitement, and worry — all normal.
- Use your calm breath, in through the nose for 4 and out for 8 through your mouth whenever you feel anxious.
- Pregnancy is a natural physiological process, not an illness.

- Begin to build your support team early: partner, family, friends, and healthcare providers.

THE ROLE OF HORMONES

Your body is now guided by a powerful hormonal orchestra that supports your pregnancy:

- hCG – sustains early pregnancy, detected by pregnancy tests, and causes morning sickness.
- Progesterone – relaxes muscles, prevents early contractions, but can slow digestion.
- Estrogen – boosts blood flow and helps your uterus and breasts grow.
- Relaxin – loosens ligaments to prepare for birth.
- Oxytocin – triggers contractions and helps bonding and breastfeeding.
- Prolactin – stimulates milk production for your baby.

DEVELOPMENTAL MILESTONES (WEEKS 1–13)

- Weeks 1–2: Your body prepares for ovulation and fertilization.
- Week 3: Conception occurs — the egg meets sperm.
- Week 4: Implantation and placenta formation begin.

- Weeks 5–8: The heart starts beating; major organs and limbs form.
- Weeks 9–13: Rapid growth; baby develops muscles, bones, nails, and hair.
- By week 13, your baby is about the size of a lemon!

COMMON FIRST TRIMESTER SYMPTOMS

- Nausea or vomiting ("morning sickness")
- Fatigue
- Breast tenderness
- Frequent urination
- Food aversions or cravings
- Lightheadedness or dizziness
- Emotional ups and downs
- Occasional spotting (light bleeding is common; seek care if heavy or painful)

Remember: Every woman's experience is unique — you may have all, some, or none of these symptoms.

MANAGING MORNING SICKNESS AND FATIGUE

- Eat small, frequent meals to keep your blood sugar stable.
- Try natural remedies such as ginger tea or acupressure wristbands.

- Rest when you can — even short naps help restore energy.
- Stay hydrated and listen to your body.
- Seek medical advice if vomiting becomes severe (possible hyperemesis gravidarum).

CHOOSING YOUR HEALTHCARE PROVIDER

- UK model: Mostly midwife-led through the NHS, with doctors only if complications arise.
- US model: Choose between OB-GYNs, family doctors, or certified nurse midwives (CNMs).
- Choose someone who listens, communicates clearly, and supports your birth preferences.
- Confirm your provider is covered by your insurance (US) or local NHS system (UK).
- Trust your instincts — you deserve care that feels respectful and calm.

NUTRITION AND SUPPLEMENTS

- Focus on whole foods: fruits, vegetables, whole grains, lean proteins.
- Hydration is essential — drink plenty of water.
- Folic acid (400–800 µg daily) before and during early pregnancy prevents neural tube defects.
- Include vitamin D and iron (if needed).

- Limit caffeine to <200 mg/day (≈ one 12 oz coffee).
- Avoid high-mercury fish, undercooked meat, and unpasteurized dairy.

YOUR FIRST PRENATAL APPOINTMENT

Usually scheduled between 8–10 weeks, it may include:

- Confirmation of pregnancy
- Review of your medical history
- Basic physical exam (no vaginal exam needed unless indicated)
- Blood and urine tests for infections, blood type, Rh status, and immunity (rubella, etc.)
- Discussion of prenatal vitamins and optional genetic testing

GENETIC TESTING OPTIONS

Screening tests (estimate risk):

- Carrier screening for inherited diseases
- First-trimester combined screening (blood + ultrasound)
- Cell-free DNA test (NIPT) for chromosomes 13, 18, 21, and sex

Diagnostic tests (confirm a diagnosis):

- CVS (10–13 weeks) or amniocentesis (15–20 weeks), if indicated

Discuss results and next steps carefully with your partner and provider.

EMOTIONAL CHANGES

- Mood swings are normal — hormones and fatigue play a big role.
- Practice 4/8 breathing, journaling, or short mindfulness sessions.
- Stay connected — share your feelings with trusted people.
- If sadness or anxiety persists, seek help; prenatal depression is treatable.
- Remember: Emotional changes are part of your transformation into motherhood.

- It is ok to have intercourse during pregnancy, reassure your partner they will not be touching or hurting the baby.

WHEN TO CALL YOUR PROVIDER

- Heavy bleeding or severe cramping
- Severe vomiting or dehydration
- Persistent headache, blurred vision, or swelling
- Painful urination with fever
- Difficulty breathing or chest pain

KEY TAKEAWAYS

- Pregnancy is a natural, physiological process, not a medical illness.
- Support, nutrition, rest, and calm breathing are your best tools right now.
- You're laying the foundation — for both your baby's growth and your own confidence as a mother.

THRIVING IN THE SECOND TRIMESTER (14-27 WEEKS)

Definition: Beginning of week 14 to 27 weeks, (4-6 months)

The second trimester is certainly a new chapter! The nausea and fatigue of the first trimester most often start to fade, giving way to a new energy and anticipation for what lies ahead. It's as if your body, having adjusted to its new role, is now ready to embrace the journey with renewed vigor. Your baby bump will well and truly make its appearance. This period is often dubbed the "honeymoon phase" of pregnancy, where many women find a comfortable rhythm as they balance the excitement and realities of their growing family. It is not the same for everyone, of course, but many people do feel a rush of energy and excitement at this stage, I know I did, and it was a great time to start thinking about what was to come. Think about what you and your partner want for your birth and also make sure to look at the calming techniques I talk about in chapter 4.

Let's first look at the facts and what is happening to your baby.

FACTS FIRST

Week 14: Your baby is about the size of your fist. Growth will start to vary baby to baby from this point on. The neck will get longer and the head becomes more upright on the torso. Hair will start to appear.

Week 15: Baby is now pear sized, can wiggle fingers and toes and even suck their thumb.

Week 16: The eyes are now in the correct position so your baby will look more recognizable. Their eyes can make some movements and perceive some light.

Week 17: Your baby has got to approximately 5 inches in length and is starting to form body fat.

Week 18: Baby has grown another half inch or so and at around 5 and a half inches, you may start to feel some movements

Week 19: Now about 6 inches long. Your baby is now covered by a protective substance called Vernix caseosa, which protects the skin from the many weeks bathed in the amniotic fluid, otherwise the skin would be very wrinkled when your baby is finally born.

Week 20: You're even more likely to feel movement now, it can feel more like a fluttering sensation or a twitch at this time. Your baby is about 6 and a half inches long. If your baby is a girl the uterus is developed now and already, remarkably, millions of primitive eggs are being held in her ovaries! The testes (balls) of male babies are beginning to descend from the abdomen.

Week 21: Rapid growth continues and your baby is likely now measuring 10.5 inches long. By this time your baby has taste buds and will be swallowing amniotic fluid which is flavored by what you eat. Arms and legs are in proportion and cartilage is turning to bone, so movements will become stronger.

Week 22: Your baby now weighs around a 1lb in weight and is at least 11 inches long. Your baby has its senses and so is hearing you and your heart beating. They are also developing a strong grip.

Week 23: Your baby is starting a time of rapid growth and weight gain, as fat deposits are forming, and their body will fill out. Right now the skin is hanging loosely as it takes longer for the fat to develop.

Week 24: Your baby is up to 1.5 pounds in weight now and is about the size of a pomegranate. The muscles, organs and bones are growing and your baby has their eyelashes and eyebrows.

Week 25: Baby is now at least 13-14 inches long and over 1.5lb in weight. The small blood vessels, capillaries, are forming all over the body and the lungs are starting to mature. The nostrils will open up this week.

Week 26: Your baby has made it to 2 lb. The eyes will begin to be open this week, the eyelids have been fused until now.

Week 27: Baby is now a good 14.6 inches long, and continues to grow steadily.

IN THIS SECOND TRIMESTER CHAPTER WE WILL DISCUSS:

- Your growing baby
- Symptoms
- Your appointments in the Second trimester
- Nutrition revisited

- Self-care tips
- Building your support network
- Partner involvement

THE GROWTH SPURT: UNDERSTANDING YOUR BABY'S DEVELOPMENT

Well, there you have it. The second trimester IS a time of rapid growth and development for your little one! Suddenly, the baby starts resembling the little human they'll become. Quite incredible how they are hearing sounds outside the womb by the middle of this trimester, and it really is amazing to be able to connect by playing your favorite music or taking them to a concert. I did that a lot and loved the idea that I had this person who was just coming with me wherever I was going, no questions asked! And when you feel them moving, you can really start to connect in a deep way.

Your body is busy adapting to this rapid growth. Your uterus expands to accommodate your growing baby, creating that baby bump you've probably been waiting for. This can cause some discomfort as ligaments stretch, but it's a sign of a healthy pregnancy. You'll also notice changes in your skin, like the linea nigra—a dark line running from your belly button to your pubic area. It's caused by hormonal changes and usually fades after birth, and is totally normal.

YOUR BODY IN THE SECOND TRIMESTER

Every pregnancy is different but generally during this trimester, nausea and vomiting should settle and although fatigue will still be present, you may find it is not as crippling as in the first months. The urinary frequency you may have experienced should also settle a little and although your breasts will continue to enlarge they may well be less painful. It can be a lovely time to bond with your baby, as many symptoms will have subsided and it is before the load becomes more cumbersome. It is an amazing time to think of the incredible work you are doing to grow your baby! Embracing your changing body is vital during this time. It's normal to experience a range of emotions about these changes. Remind yourself daily that your body is doing something amazing. Dress in comfortable, flattering maternity wear that makes you feel good about yourself. Whether it's a cozy pair of leggings or a stylish maternity top, wearing clothes that accommodate your growing bump can enhance your comfort and self-esteem.

I am not saying it is all going to be plain sailing. We will all get various symptoms at times, but in a normal pregnancy, this is a time to enjoy-I genuinely loved being pregnant and this second trimester was an energizing time for me-it can almost give you an extra boost of energy that you can use to your advantage as you starting planning for the future with your baby and thinking about getting your home ready.

You might feel like being more active in this trimester and I can't encourage this enough. The more active you stay in pregnancy, the more easily you can adjust to the changes taking place in your body. One friend remarked that she was not quite prepared for quite how much her body would change. It's true, it can be a huge adjustment, but keeping some of your exercise routines and generally active can really help with this process. It will likely improve your energy and reduce fatigue and can help prepare you for labor. Walking, swimming, yoga, pilates, low-impact aerobics and cycling (stationary better later in pregnancy) can all be beneficial, and lift your mood with the release of endorphins. It is also never too early to start pelvic floor exercises which strengthen the muscles that support the uterus and bladder, and can help with labor and recovery.

Of course, your body is dealing with a lot and not everything for everyone goes right. This is a small concise book about pregnancy and cannot cover all eventualities in detail but here I have mentioned common second trimester symptoms and two of the main possible complications that can occur or begin in this trimester.

NB: As you go through this trimester don't forget to keep writing down any thoughts or worries week to week in the notes section at the back. That way, it will remind you to mention it to your provider at your next visit, or not, if the symptom subsides. Many of these symptoms are all part of the body preparing for birth and growing your baby.

Here are the some of the symptoms this trimester may bring:

Fatigue: your body is doing a lot so this isn't surprising. Take short naps if you can during the day, but the rest of the time keep your body moving and active, de-stress with some quick breathwork, remember 4/8 breathing, and eat dinner on the early side, all of which should help you sleep better at night, to help with the increased fatigue. Most friends I spoke to when preparing to write this book, in asking their key takeaways from their pregnancies was: Rest, rest, rest! One said "I could not believe the exhaustion that came from making another whole person, I would often nap on the examination couch!" Take the opportunity to rest when you can.

Abdominal Symptoms: including constipation, heartburn, indigestion, wind, bloating. Again these hormonal changes I keep mentioning, in this case, progesterone and relaxin (the one that softens the ligaments), can relax the smooth muscle in your gastrointestinal tract (where your food goes), making digestion slower. These symptoms may be uncomfortable at times, but think of it as a benefit for your baby-slower digestion, more time for nutrients to be absorbed into your blood stream as the food passes through, therefore more good stuff being channeled to the placenta and ultimately your baby. I get that you're perhaps not thinking along those lines where you're experiencing this kind of discomfort but try these tips to help and talk to your HCP if its not controllable: more often and smaller meals during the day, avoid spicy, citrus, fried foods and any others that seem to trigger the symptoms, eat slowly and have your liquids between meals rather than with, having lots of water with the meal can cause too much stomach expansion which can increase symptoms. But make sure to keep drinking plenty!

Lightheadedness/dizziness: especially if you stand from sitting/change position quickly. Hormonal changes mean your blood vessels widen and relax more during pregnancy, to increase blood flow to your baby, but in turn this means slower blood flow back to your heart. So try not to move too quickly so the body has time to adjust. Also keep a small nutritious snack with you in case this feeling is caused by low blood sugar.

Nasal congestion: with the increase in circulating blood that we talked about earlier, mucus membranes will swell, including those in your nose, causing stuffiness and even sometimes nose bleeds. Saline sprays are safe and fine to use; a humidifier may help a bit. If you do get a nose bleed, lean slightly forward and pinch the soft part of your nose for at least 5 minutes.

Bleeding gums: for the same reason, this swelling of the mucus membranes in your body will cause your gums to swell, and sometimes bleed. Make sure you practice good dental hygiene, with flossing included, during pregnancy.

Mild swelling of feet/ankles (see also pre-eclampsia): this increased blood volume I keep talking about and hormonal changes, and pressure from the growing uterus on blood vessels in the lower legs, will likely cause some mild ankle and foot swelling. Your HCP will monitor this in your visits. Remain active, wear comfortable shoes, and elevate your legs when you're sitting. Activity will improve blood circulation, helping the extra blood volume work its way back to the heart. Lymphatic fluid can pool in the lower legs and ankles if you're sitting or standing for long periods-using your muscles and moving your joints will help move this fluid back towards your chest.

Increased appetite: this is all part of the process, particularly in the 2nd trimester when we know the organs are generally formed and your baby is growing in size. Try to supplement those calories as much as possible with nutrient rich foods, better fats such as olive oil, avocado, nuts, seeds, and try to limit the ultra-processed (as always) and 'junk foods' which are really calories that don't count in terms of being nutritious for you and your baby. See more in the nutrition section. Cravings can come into play-carrying my son, it was salty chips/crisps, but particularly with my first daughter I found myself buying bags of candy, something I had never done before. Just limit those if you can.

Mood swings: you have a lot going on. Your body is doing stirling work, and your hormone levels have changed. Swings may be more pronounced, you may find yourself in floods of tears over something that would not normally bother you. Yup! Use your support network, your partner, your friends, make sure to talk out your worries, journal, breathe (remember the 4/8 breath). If you are finding your anxieties and your mood harder and harder to control, please talk to your HCP. You may need extra support.

Headaches: And another one. This was one of my main symptoms, but they are something I've always been prone to. And of course you need to take more care in what you take for them. Ibuprofen/

advil is off limits here, but acetaminophen/ tylenol/paracetamol are all ok. Try to lie in a darkened room with your eyes shut for even 5 minutes (ideally 20) and do your 4/8 breath when you have a headache, drink plenty of water, and eat your regular meals.

Backache: ligaments are relaxing due to hormonal changes, particularly in the pelvic area, part of the body's preparation for your baby's passage through the birth canal.

Increased vaginal discharge: this is normal and the body's way of protecting the birth canal from infection. If it starts to smell, that's a time to talk to your healthcare provider.

Leg cramps: these can increase in the 2nd and 3rd trimesters and we don't really know why. Hormones are probably our best bet here, as the pattern shows. We all know how agonizing cramps can be. Straighten your leg and flex your foot upwards (ie not pointing it away), massage it, a heat pad may help. Keep drinking fluids.

Varicose veins: as we talked about, blood volume increases substantially during pregnancy, and this pressure on your blood vessels, especially those in your legs, where they are working against gravity as well as the uterus pressing down on your pelvic veins and the hormones relaxing the blood vessels, it's really like a perfect storm! But it doesn't actually affect everyone. It can cause aching in the legs. Keep active, don't do any heavy lifting or strain during bowel movements and wear support stockings if you can.

Haemorrhoids (piles): It's a similar situation with these, I'm afraid. Increased blood volume, swollen veins in the rectum due to pressure of the uterus on them. Annoyingly they can itch and bulge. This did not escape me, super annoying! Sitting on a bag of ice (more on that after delivery!), don't strain when you are taking a bowel movement, and keep water intake and fiber up (see also nutrition section).

Skin changes: we've talked about the linea nigra, a line of darker skin that can appear from your tummy button to your pubic area. You can also develop melasma, which are areas of dark or lighter brown areas on your face. They are more pronounced if you have darker skin. They are a result of hormone changes and genetic factors.

I have to explain that this is not an exhaustive list. This concise book is giving you the main standout symptoms that may occur. Remember to always discuss with your pharmacist or HCP before you take any medications to relieve symptoms of pregnancy. Some are off limits for pregnancy as they can cross the placenta.

In happier news, your hair will grow like never before and be thicker and more lustrous, your nails will grow apace, and fun fact, you might increase a shoe size! Again related to the ligaments relaxing that we talked about above, so the foot bones can spread and may well be a permanent change. I see a new shoe collection in your future. Hold on to these less daunting facts about pregnancy!

YOUR APPOINTMENTS IN THIS TRIMESTER

Regular checks of:

- Fundal height (growth-measured from top of pubic bone to the top of uterus-from about 20 weeks this measurement in cm should equal the number of weeks you are ±2cm)
- Blood pressure
- Urine,
- Heart beat,
- Any swelling of hands/feet
- Symptoms as above!
- Questions, remember to check your notes
- Weight (this can be avoided after an initial weigh, unless it is needed for care)

A note about '**baby weight**': remember you're carrying the baby, the placenta, increased fluid around the baby (amniotic fluid), increased breast tissue, a higher blood volume, extra fluid retention, and more fat stores. Try not to get hung up on numbers. There is no perfect weight gain but most women will gain at least between 22-30 lb but there is no exact number for anyone. Week-to-week swings are also normal (fluid, salt, constipation), so don't judge yourself by a single weigh-in and try to avoid weigh-ins yourself. What matters most is how you and your baby are growing—your HCP tracks this with fundal height and scans, not with the scale. Focus on habits you can control which we will talk about in the nutrition section: regular meals and snacks, plenty of protein, fruit/veg, whole grains, and staying hydrated. Gentle movement (walks, stretching, yoga) and sleep help more than strict rules. Be kind to yourself most importantly. You're doing a lot, and your body knows a lot about how to do this.

The key anatomy scan around 20 weeks is a detailed ultrasound that checks your baby's organs and measures growth. It's a chance to see your baby in detail and confirm their sex if you choose. It is a detailed scan scheduled at this time once all organs and features are developed and now growing rather than forming, so any abnormalities should be picked up at this time.

Another important test during this trimester is screening for **gestational diabetes**, which helps ensure both your health and your baby's. A note on Gestational Diabetes (GD). This is a form of diabetes that only occurs in pregnancy, (when blood sugar levels are generally higher due to hormonal changes), where the body becomes more resistant to insulin, the hormone in your body that controls your blood sugar levels. Screening for this is done in the 2nd trimester because if you're going to get it, onset is usually from 24 to 28 weeks. It can affect 2-10% of mothers. Screening involves having a blood sample taken an hour after drinking a very sweet drink. If the glucose numbers in the blood test are high then you will need to have what's called a Glucose Tolerance Test (GTT) which can actually diagnose GD. This involves fasting before being given the sugar load and then blood tests to check how your body deals with the sugar. If you do have GD, the important thing to note is that if your diet is well controlled (your doctor will likely make some changes) and your pregnancy carefully monitored, then your pregnancy is likely to progress normally and your baby will be healthy. Occasionally women will need to take insulin. In this case in the UK, you would likely be referred to a specialist at the hospital. The likelihood of GD developing in pregnancy, in the US and Europe, is around 7-8% of pregnancies.

A note about GD: when the body becomes resistant to insulin, it can affect the development of the milk producing cells in the breasts leading to possible lower colostrum/ milk production in the first 72 hours after birth. Mothers can express and store some colostrum before birth to then give to baby in those first few days to stabilize baby's blood sugar.

I've also mentioned the phrase **pre-eclampsia** and I want to explain a little about this, before we continue. Many of the tests done at your pre-natal checks at this time and in later pregnancy are informed by checking that you are not developing this condition. Pre-eclampsia is one of the most common pregnancy complications and it can start to develop in the 2nd trimester. It can affect 5-8% of pregnancies worldwide and early detection is the key to a good outcome for mother and baby. The cause of the condition is not really known although it may be related to blood supply to the placenta. It is characterized by high blood pressure and protein in the urine (proteinuria). Untreated, the condition puts stress on your major organs like the kidneys, heart, lungs and liver so that is why it is essential to attend all your prenatal health checks and let your HCP know if something changes. Women can also suffer with headaches and blurred vision. You may, however, not be aware or feel any different early on, so checking blood pressure and urine is important for tell-tale signs. You can't really pinpoint who might get it, but you would have extra risk if: a) you have a history of high blood pressure, kidney problems or diabetes, or b) if you're carrying more than one baby, c) if you have certain autoimmune conditions or you've had it in a previous pregnancy. If it is left untreated it can be very serious, but if there are any signs, your HCP will do extra tests and keep a close eye on you. There is no specific drug treatment. Your HCP will watch and monitor you. The only actual cure is delivering the baby but this is a balancing act as your HCP will want the baby to be as strong as possible before delivery, and in particular a baby's lungs are still maturing close to 37 weeks, but medications can be given to help with that if it seems likely you will need an earlier delivery.

Of course, in a larger more comprehensive reference book, there are many other, more rare complications of pregnancy, and this book does not hold the scope to mention all of these, nor would it be helpful, as most of them you will never even hear about let alone have, but these both are more common and because of that it's important to explain them so you understand.

NUTRITION REVISITED: ADJUSTING YOUR DIET FOR THE SECOND TRIMESTER

As your pregnancy progresses into the second trimester, your body's nutritional needs evolve, demanding a bit more attention. Caloric intake naturally increases during this phase, with about 340 extra calories needed daily to support fetal development. These aren't just any calories, though. Focus on nutrient-rich foods that offer real benefits. Think whole grains, lean proteins, and colorful fruits and veggies. This isn't about doubling your portions but making smart choices that nourish both you and your baby. As you gain weight, remember it's not just extra pounds: you're carrying the baby, the placenta, increased fluid around the baby (amniotic fluid), increased breast tissue, a higher blood volume, extra fluid retention, and more fat stores

Iron becomes a key player in your diet now. It helps prevent anemia, which, if left unchecked, can leave you feeling even more exhausted. Foods like spinach, lentils, and lean beef are great sources. If you're vegetarian or vegan, pair plant-based iron sources with vitamin C-rich foods like oranges or bell peppers to boost absorption. It's all about creating a balanced plate that keeps your energy up and your body strong.

Meal planning becomes your ally in this. Instead of scrambling for meals, and believe me, I know this is easier said than done, and some weeks are better than others, but try setting aside time to plan ahead. You could even try batch cooking at the weekend, which can be a lifesaver for busy weeks. Think about preparing a variety of dishes that include grains, proteins, and vegetables. For those dealing with dietary restrictions like gluten or dairy intolerances, focus on naturally gluten-free grains like quinoa or rice. With vegetarian or vegan diets, ensure you're getting enough protein through beans, lentils, tofu, or tempeh. These diets can be fulfilling and diverse if you keep your pantry stocked with the right ingredients.

Hydration takes center stage too. As your blood volume increases, so does the need for fluids. Aim for eight to ten cups of fluid daily to keep everything running smoothly. Water is essential, but herbal teas or diluted fruit juices can add variety without unnecessary sugars. Keeping a water bottle with you at all times is a simple way to remind yourself to sip regularly. You can always flavour it with some citrus or cucumber, or drink coconut or flavored waters for variety.

Snacking smartly can also help meet your nutritional needs while keeping hunger at bay. Opt for nutrient-dense options like nuts, yoghurt, or fresh fruit. These snacks are easy to grab when you're on the go and offer an energy boost without the crash. Nuts provide healthy fats and protein, yoghurt offers calcium and probiotics, and fruits deliver vitamins and fiber.

Remember, it's perfectly fine to indulge cravings now and then as long as you're mindful of overall balance. Pregnancy is a time of change and adaptation, so listen to your body's cues and respond with kindness and understanding. You're doing something amazing, and good nourishment is key. Tuning into what fuels you best not only supports your baby's growth but enhances your pregnancy experience.

Lastly, don't hesitate to consult with a healthcare provider if you have questions about your diet. Make notes in the back to discuss at your next visit. They can provide tailored advice based on your individual needs. It's about finding what works for you and embracing the journey of nourishing yourself and your little one together.

EMBRACING YOUR CHANGING BODY: SELF-CARE TIPS

Pregnancy brings about an incredible transformation, and embracing these changes is key to a positive experience. Fostering a mindset of body positivity and self-love can make all the difference. You can even try practicing positive affirmations. Stand in front of the mirror each morning and remind yourself of your strength and beauty. Simple statements like "I am strong" or "My body is creating life" can uplift your spirits and reinforce a positive outlook. Give it a try if you don't already do it. Or you could even write in your journal three things you are grateful for, before you get out of bed in the morning. Complement these practices by dressing in comfortable yet flattering maternity wear. Choosing clothes that make you feel good about yourself can boost your confidence and help you celebrate your evolving form.

Incorporating practical self-care routines into your daily life can further enhance your well-being during pregnancy. Prenatal yoga offers gentle stretching and strengthening exercises that are tailored to support your body as it adapts. It provides not only physical benefits but also a mental escape, allowing you to connect with your body and your baby. Even if yoga isn't your thing, consider incorporating simple stretching exercises into your routine. They can be done in the comfort of your home and require minimal equipment.

Warm baths with Epsom salts are another way to promote relaxation and muscle relief. The soothing warmth of the water can help alleviate tension in your muscles, while Epsom salts offer a gentle detoxifying effect. It's a simple indulgence that can leave you feeling refreshed and rejuvenated. Just remember to keep the water at a comfortable temperature and avoid long soaks to prevent overheating. I am not a big swimmer but found great relief in the local swimming pool while pregnant, for the same reasons.

Managing common discomforts is a part of the pregnancy experience, but there are at least some solutions to help you stay comfortable and mobile. Back pain is a common complaint, often due to the shift in your center of gravity as your belly grows. Practicing good posture, using supportive pillows while sitting or sleeping, making sure there is a 90 degree angle at your knees if sitting at a desk for long hours, and wearing comfortable shoes, can make a big difference. If back pain persists, consider seeking advice from a physical therapist who specializes in prenatal care.

Some of the other symptoms we've talked about in this chapter, like leg cramps and swelling, are other typical discomforts during pregnancy. These can be minimized by staying hydrated, engaging in regular gentle exercise, and elevating your legs whenever possible. If leg cramps strike at night, try stretching your calves before bed or massaging them gently to relieve tension.

Pampering yourself isn't just a luxury—it's a necessity during pregnancy. If within your budget, scheduling regular prenatal massages can ease muscle tension and improve circulation, providing both physical relief and emotional relaxation. It's an opportunity to unwind and let someone else take care of you for a change. Additionally, setting aside time for hobbies and relaxation is essential. Whether it's painting, knitting, or simply reading a good book, or going on a neighborhood walk, immersing yourself in activities you love can be a wonderful way to recharge and enjoy this unique phase of life.

Taking time for self-care not only nurtures your body but also strengthens the bond with your baby. By embracing these practices, you are giving yourself permission to prioritize your well-being, ensuring that you approach each day with energy and positivity. And never forget the 4/8 breath, you can use it every day, and that practice will be key, as we will find out in Chapter 4, as delivery day approaches.

A quick note on YOUR body as your lovely baby bump develops in this 2nd trimester. YOUR is the operative word, but plenty of people, for some reason, will feel some entitlement to touching your baby bump. Tempting, yes, but really not ok. You would not go up to someone and rub their tummy, but, if you think about it, that is basically what they are doing. You can politely put your hand out to stop them, and say any number of things like "I'd rather you didn't" or "No, baby is sleeping now" or something more inspired! Just know it will happen, so be prepared with your come back if it is something you don't want.

BUILDING YOUR SUPPORT NETWORK: WHO TO INCLUDE

I cannot express this enough. Building a support network becomes increasingly important as you settle into the second trimester. Your partner, family members, and close friends are likely to form the core of this group. Their involvement provides emotional support and practical assistance as you prepare for your baby's arrival.

Whether it's your mother sharing her own experiences or siblings pitching in with day-to-day chores, their presence can provide comfort and reassurance. I am also well aware, as I now live thousands of miles from my Mum and siblings, that they may only be at the end of the telephone. For my first baby, for 6 months after he was born, it was the one time both my sisters lived within 20 minutes of me in London, and I will never forget it, that feeling of support and togetherness that family brings was so special. That's why sometimes, in this world where in Western culture particularly, women often move far away from family, we have to get creative with our support networks. Trust me you need it, so look out for any groups of pregnant women and your local friends, if family are not nearby or they are not the most supportive or understanding.

Friends who've been through pregnancy themselves bring an added layer of understanding. They know the highs and lows and can offer practical advice, from what to pack in your hospital bag to soothing remedies for morning sickness. Just a word of advice on family and friends. You do not want to be filled with negative birth stories, more on this later, but if that seems to be coming, politely decline to hear that story until after your birth. These stories can have a negative impact and you really want to fill up with positive stories right now.

Connecting with other expectant mothers can also be invaluable. Joining local or online pregnancy groups offers a sense of community where shared experiences foster understanding and camaraderie. In the UK, for my first child's birth, I joined the National Childbirth Trust, an organisation that offers prenatal classes, a series of 6-8 I seem to remember. The key to its success, for me, and many others I have talked to, was that they grouped women together by location and due date, and what an inspired thing to do. These 7 special women have now been my friends for 21 years, our first children just reached that milestone. We gradually had our babies and met up regularly, saw each other through the ups and downs, breastfeeding issues, relationship issues, fussy babies and sleepless nights, developmental problems, you name it. And we still do meet, even on zoom as we are now spread from Scotland to Suffolk and London, Sydney and Los Angeles. Devastatingly, we lost one of our group a few months ago. This book is dedicated to her and this powerhouse of women.

Regular check-ins with your doctor or midwife ensure that both you and your baby are thriving. They offer expertise and guidance tailored to your needs, from prenatal nutrition to managing unexpected symptoms. Also remember that this is a physiological process, not a medical condition or disease. Your body was designed for this.

During this time you can also consider hiring a doula for your birth. Doulas offer physical and emotional support during labor, helping you stay calm and focused. Their presence can be incredibly reassuring, especially if you're feeling anxious about childbirth (more about this in Chapter 5).

Online forums and social media groups connect you with people worldwide who share similar due dates or experiences. There is a wealth of information and shared knowledge out there. You'll find everything from product recommendations to advice on dealing with in-laws who overstay their welcome. These platforms often allow you to ask questions, share your story, and gain support at any hour of the day or night. Whether you're seeking advice on choosing a crib or need reassurance about an unusual pregnancy symptom, there's always someone ready to help. Don't forget to filter out the negative stories. And I would also caution you here. Much of the information out there is not checked or edited, and may not be right for you.

Move towards people you trust, likely with your partner at the core. I would even say, a small group of trusted people is better than all the social media noise, it can become loud and overwhelming and take your focus away from the job at hand.

PARTNER INVOLVEMENT: STRENGTHENING YOUR RELATIONSHIP

Partner involvement deepens during this stage, strengthening your relationship as you prepare for parenthood together. Attend prenatal appointments as a team. It's a time for you both to ask questions. Making sure your partner feels just as involved as you, in decision making and support.

Attending prenatal classes together with your partner offers dual benefits. Not only do you gain valuable insights into childbirth and baby care, but you also strengthen your relationship through shared learning experiences.

These classes cover topics like labor positions, breathing techniques, and newborn care basics—knowledge that empowers both partners as they prepare for parenthood. And you can then develop your plan for the birth and beyond with shared knowledge. The classes I talked about earlier were all for partners to attend also and it really was essential to the shared experience.

Finding activities that enhance your connection can strengthen your relationship during pregnancy. Couples prenatal yoga classes offer not only physical benefits but also a chance to relax and connect on a deeper level. These classes encourage you to work together, supporting each other through poses and breathing exercises. Evening walks provide a calm setting to unwind and discuss your day, strengthening your emotional connection. Shared relaxation time, whether it's watching a favorite movie or enjoying a quiet dinner, reinforces your partnership and reminds you of the love that brought you together.

Navigating relationship changes and expectations during pregnancy requires open communication. It's natural for dynamics to shift as you prepare for parenthood. Discussing your fears and expectations openly can prevent misunderstandings and ensure you're on the same page. Set shared goals and responsibilities, dividing tasks in a way that feels fair and manageable for both of you. Your partner might want to research the best car seats or even make up the crib. There are plenty of ways to feel involved.

This partnership approach not only eases the load but also reinforces the idea that you're in this together.

Talk about your birth wishes and expectations together, considering what's most important for each of you during labor and delivery. Discuss parenting styles and values, exploring how you want to raise your child and what principles matter most to you both.

WHERE TO HAVE MY BABY

This is one of those important discussions you have probably already had and made a decision on, but before we enter the third trimester we need to make sure you have considered this thoroughly and that you and your partner are happy with the decision you have made.

Whether you're planning a home birth, heading to a birthing center, or preparing for a hospital delivery, understanding the protocols and procedures can ease your mind and help you focus on the experience. Each setting offers unique environments and procedures, so familiarize yourself with what each option entails. This knowledge empowers you to make decisions that align with your preferences and ensures you're not caught off guard when the big day arrives.

If you've opted for a home birth, the comfort of familiar surroundings can create a sense of tranquility. Discuss the logistics with your midwife or healthcare provider well in advance. Knowing which room you'll use and having a plan for any unexpected scenarios is key. Your midwife will make sure you have a birth kit ready with necessary supplies and ensure your home is equipped with appropriate safety measures. If complications arise, have a clear plan for transferring to a hospital if needed.

Communication with your support team is crucial, ensuring everyone knows their roles and responsibilities. Research suggests that a planned home birth in a low risk pregnancy, results in fewer interventions, including epidural and caesarean sections and fewer perineal tears.

It is essential to ensure that timely transfer to a medical facility would be possible in case of complications. In 2020, the Lancet, a world-renowned medical journal out of the UK did what's called a meta-analysis of data, meaning they analysed a number of studies to see what conclusions it came to. They looked at 16 studies that involved 500,000 women. Conclusions reported no maternal deaths, and no higher rates of perinatal death in newborns, and a lower rate of induction, episiotomy, Caesarean section, 3rd or 4th degree tears, maternal infection and epidural in home births. The National Institutes of Health report a study of 63,000 births in the USA which showed exactly the same results, conducted due to lingering doubts about home birth in the USA. 1 in 50 births in the USA are now either birth center or home deliveries and the results above suggest strongly that in low risk pregnancies with experienced midwives (who, as we have already discussed, are experts in natural birth) this is an excellent option with far fewer interventions for women. However the American College of Obstetricians and Gynecologists ACOG) still do not recommend it, in opposition to both the American College of Nurse-Midwives and the National Academy of Medicine. It is interesting to note that the ACOG base their conclusions on birth certificate data, and they do not include the planned place of birth of infants so data is skewed by unplanned home births being combined with planned, and hospital births with transfers during labor.

For those choosing a birthing center, it's essential to understand their specific protocols. Birthing centers provide a home-like environment with professional support. They often focus on natural childbirth, offering amenities like birthing tubs and comfortable rooms. Before labor begins, take a tour to familiarize yourself with the facilities and meet the staff. Knowing the admissions procedure can alleviate stress, allowing you to concentrate on the moment rather than logistics. Birthing centers typically have transfer agreements with nearby hospitals in case medical intervention becomes necessary, so stay informed about what steps will be taken if this occurs. My birthing center, for my first two children, was attached to a hospital so when I needed more monitoring with my second, it was a question of walking down the corridor. The evidence and studies confirm that birthing center deliveries also significantly reduce all complications listed above-maternal deaths, perinatal death in newborns, induction, episiotomy, Caesarean section, 3rd or 4th degree tears, maternal infection and epidural.

Hospital births offer access to comprehensive medical care, making them a preferred choice for many. Each hospital has its own set of procedures, so attending an informational session or hospital tour is beneficial. Learn about their admission process—knowing where to go and who to contact can make all the difference when labor begins. Hospitals provide a structured environment with immediate access to medical interventions if needed. They may have specific policies regarding visitors and pain management options, so it's crucial to discuss these in advance with your healthcare provider. The vast majority of births take place in hospitals in the UK and USA.

I have to mention a rather shocking statistic here, which I would be remiss to leave out of a book on pregnancy and childbirth. Maternal Mortality is the record of deaths of mothers either during childbirth or within the first 42 days after delivery. The rate in the USA is 22 deaths per 100,000 live births and has been increasing since 2000, along with only 7 other countries, whereas in the UK it is 5.5 and has been relatively stable at that level for some time. The US rate is actually much higher than all developed countries despite spending vastly more on healthcare than all these countries. The maternal mortality rate in the USA, unlike the UK, is skewed to low income mothers, those in rural areas, and there is also a higher incidence in black mothers compared to white or Hispanic women. Causes are mixed but include heart conditions, blood clots, bleeding, infection and stroke. It underscores the need for excellence in health care for mothers prenatally, during delivery and postpartum. Trust your instincts and try to surround yourself with providers who don't overcomplicate this natural process, and always feel empowered to ask questions. Any provider who does not like your questions is a red flag. Answering your questions and feeling comfortable asking why is crucial in this process.

Understanding the admissions procedure for your chosen place of birth is vital. Whether you're headed to a birthing center or hospital, have your documentation ready—identification, insurance information, and birth plan, are essential. Knowing what paperwork to complete beforehand can save time and reduce anxiety when things start moving quickly. Some facilities offer online registration to streamline the process, so inquire whether this is an option.

This brings up a vital issue for discussion. Systemic racism in maternity care leads to unequal care and outcomes for people from racial and ethnic minority groups, particularly Black women, and this is regardless of income and education. Causes include implicit bias, poor access to quality care, and under-listening to concerns, particularly around pain. As a result Black women are significantly (2.5

to 3.5 times) more likely to experience severe complications and maternal death in both the US and the UK, although overall numbers are much lower in the UK as maternal mortality is much lower, as detailed earlier. Both countries have programs in place to combat these worrying trends. Amongst other initiatives, the CDC (Centers for Disease Control) set up the ERASE Maternal Mortality program and the 'Hear Her' campaign to raise awareness and warning signs in pregnancy and postpartum care and in the UK, the National Health Service (NHS) set up the Maternity Disparities Taskforce to explore and address these poorer outcomes in women from ethnic minorities.

Chapter 3 Checklist:

THE BIG PICTURE

- Often the "honeymoon phase": nausea eases, energy returns, bump appears.
- Great time to start shaping your **birth preferences/plan** and practicing **calm breathing**.

BABY'S GROWTH (HIGHLIGHTS)

- Rapid growth in size, fat deposition, and movement ("quickening" usually by ~18–20 wks).
- Senses develop: hearing by mid-trimester; swallowing amniotic fluid; taste buds active.

- 20-week anatomy scan checks organs, placenta, cord, and growth.

HOW YOU MIGHT FEEL

- Common improvements: less nausea, steadier energy, fewer bathroom trips (for now).
- Normal symptoms: heartburn/indigestion, constipation, dizziness, blocked nose, gum bleeding, headaches, backache, leg cramps, varicose veins/hemorrhoids, increased discharge, mild ankle/foot swelling.
- Skin changes (linea nigra, melasma) are common and usually fade postpartum.

SELF-CARE & EVERYDAY TIPS

- Eat **small, frequent meals**; sip fluids between meals for reflux.
- Keep moving: walking, prenatal yoga, gentle stretching; short daytime rests if needed.
- Support posture (pillows, chair setup, flat shoes); stretch calves to prevent cramps.
- Practice **4/8 breathing** daily; brief mindfulness or journaling helps mood.
- Dress for comfort and confidence; embrace body changes.

NUTRITION REFRESH

- About **+340 kcal/day** on average; prioritize nutrient density over portion size.
- Focus: protein, iron (pair plant iron with vitamin C), calcium, fiber, healthy fats.
- Hydration: aim ~8–10 cups fluids/day.
- Continue prenatal: **folic acid, vitamin D, iron if indicated**.
- Limit caffeine to **<200 mg/day**; avoid high-mercury fish and unpasteurized foods.

APPOINTMENTS & SCREENING

- Routine checks: **fundal height**, blood pressure, urine, fetal heart, swelling, symptoms.
- **20-week anatomy scan** (detailed ultrasound).
- **Gestational diabetes screening** typically **24–28 weeks** (glucose challenge; GTT if needed).

WATCHOUTS: TWO KEY CONDITIONS

- **Pre-eclampsia**: monitor BP/urine; report headaches, visual changes, sudden swelling.
- **Gestational diabetes**: screening is standard; diet + monitoring usually effective.

BUILDING YOUR SUPPORT NETWORK

- Nurture a small, trusted circle (partner, friends, local/online groups, classes).
- Consider a **doula** for continuous labor support.
- Filter out **negative birth stories**; protect your calm.

PARTNER INVOLVEMENT

- Attend appointments/classes together; share decisions and preparation tasks.
- Try couples' routines (evening walks, prenatal yoga, relaxation practice).

PLANNING WHERE TO GIVE BIRTH

- Explore **home, birth center, or hospital** based on risks, preferences, and local resources.
- Tour facilities; understand admission steps, transfer plans, and policies.
- Start drafting your **birth preferences** for discussion in the next chapter.

WHEN TO CONTACT YOUR PROVIDER (SECOND TRIMESTER)

- Vaginal bleeding, leaking fluid, or painful contractions.

- Persistent severe headache, vision changes, right-upper-abdominal pain, sudden swelling.
- Fever, painful urination, reduced fetal movement after you've been feeling regular movements.
- Severe, unrelenting vomiting or signs of dehydration.

CALM, CONFIDENT MINDSET

- This is still a **natural, physiological process**.
- Your daily toolkit: **regular meals, hydration, gentle movement, rest, and the calm breath**.

Note: I am hearing from clients in the USA that ultrasounds are performed more often in prenatal care, often to estimate baby weight. I would avoid these extra ultrasounds if possible. Often women are scanned early in pregnancy to establish a viable pregnancy with a heart beat and to check dates, but apart from this the only scan you need is the 20 week anatomy scan, and I would avoid all others. Further scans involving predicted baby weight which is often inaccurate, is just one more thing to breed fear, and I am determined to reduce that as much as I can.

We will now move on to our crucial central chapter on calm birthing techniques and then on to the 3rd trimester.

CHAPTER 4

THE ART OF CALM BIRTHING TECHNIQUES EXPLAINED

This chapter is dear to my heart. And essential reading for anyone who plans to have as natural a birth as possible. I owe it to my sister that my awareness and knowledge of these techniques is now at the forefront of my mind as I write this book. She is a HypnoBirthing® teacher and has taught me her course. I did manage to have 3 unmedicated deliveries, including one with an induction (more on that later) but would have loved to have added in some of these techniques, or at least have had a more formal training of them. I purely went on instinct, moved in rhythm when it felt right, made quite loud low animalistic sounds at later points and wasn't quiet, but got through it as I had decided a) I did not want anyone sticking a needle in my back (from years of back pain related to scoliosis this was something

I hated the idea of) and b) I didn't want anyone cutting through muscles in my abdomen that I had spent years building up to be able to sing with support.

Just a quick note before we continue with this chapter. HypnoBirthing® is a registered trademark of the HypnoBirthing Institute. In this chapter I talk about ideas and methods related to that technique that I find helpful in coaching mothers for birth.

One of the big takeaways from this course for me, in hearing my sister's birth stories through hypnobirthing and watching videos of deliveries using these techniques, was that these deliveries took place with mothers in a state of deep relaxation. They were often very quiet. Partners were also quiet, and took cues from their partner's movements and gestures. They were in tune. Hypnobirthing techniques are shown to decrease interventions in labor, decrease the need for pain medications and decrease the likelihood of cesarean birth.

To me and the best way for me to explain to you, these women were not 'hypnotized' per se, not in the way you might have seen someone being put in a trance with a pendulum. They were deeply relaxed. Their body was fully engaged in the 'job' of labor, signs were observed and progression was steady. There was no fear in this process. It was a surrender to what our bodies know what to do. It was beautiful.

In western medicine, and in some countries more than others, we have stepped so far away from this process, that even women themselves are losing their power to believe. This is a true sadness to me, and the reason I started writing about it, something I have wanted to do since I moved to the United States and started talking to mothers and hearing birth stories. The fear was palpable. They were no longer trusting their bodies. It is the reason I have now trained as a doula. Women need advocates in this space, to get back to what we were made to do. Women are underestimated. We are powerful, strong, and physiologically designed for this process, and I believe that using these techniques will help you to have the birth experience you want to have, whatever it ends up being in the moment, even that Caesarean section you were perhaps desperately trying to avoid. You can still use these techniques. Cesareans can be calm and woman-centered too. Sometimes, intervention is just unavoidable-after all, our ultimate aim is to have a healthy baby, and bodies and babies don't always cooperate with our plans.

FEAR-TENSION-PAIN

This is crucial to understand before we move on to techniques. This triad moving from fear, to tension to pain sums it up.

This triad of fear-tension-pain was first coined by the British Obstetrician Grantly Dick-Read. Fun fact being that he was my grandmother's obstetrician just before the second world war, in the late 1930's, when my Mum was born. In 1942 he wrote the paper "Childbirth Without Fear". He recognised that when babies were born at home, in their natural environment, they tended to have quieter, natural births, whereas the women who went into hospital, which was becoming more common in those days, tended to scream and cry. This was revolutionary in the birthing space. He observed and concluded that the fear these women felt, being in an unfamiliar environment, probably also with less of their support people around, became tense and this then increased the pain they felt during childbirth, leading to an inability to cope with contractions, an overwhelm, if you like, which led to more complications and intervention.

This is what I see and hear about in many birth stories, particularly in the US, where the hospital system is set up for intervention.

To name but a few, women are generally put in a bed when they arrive at the hospital, when remaining mobile is so important in labor, epidurals are often offered early, and, what you may not know is that if you have one, you are then not able to leave the bed, and often have a tube placed in your bladder, as the epidural leaves you unable to feel the lower half of your body, so it is not safe to try walking to the restroom/toilet. There is a sense that time is an issue so augmentation of labor with medication (typically

Pitocin) is commonly used, which can often 'ramp up' a labor very quickly, which can be fear-inducing and scary. The lights are bright, the rooms are cold so that equipment works efficiently, and there are often numerous people in the room. I am not saying that these things are universal -some inductions can be slowly and carefully managed, some hospitals will allow more leeway with labor slowing down-but it certainly can be like this.

HOW OUR MIND CAN HELP

You may have heard the term 'subconscious'. In fact the mind, simply put, is split into three parts:

The conscious mind is what you're aware of right now. It's your thinking, decision making, focusing and reasoning, like deciding what to eat for dinner, working out how to solve that math problem, or remembering someone's name.

The subconscious mind is like the 'middle layer', just below awareness. It stores habits, beliefs, memories, feelings and automatic skills. Like riding a bike, once you've learned you don't consciously think about balancing any more, your subconscious is guiding you. It is active when we dream, and also can be associated with flashes of creativity.

The unconscious mind is the deepest layer, fully outside of our awareness. It controls automatic bodily functions like breathing, digestion, and our heart beat, and also holds hidden memories or instincts.

The idea in calm birthing (giving birth in a deeply relaxed state) is that we are allowing the **subconscious mind** to do the work it knows how to do, where we are not 'overthinking' but letting the instincts and trust of our own body to take over.

The subconscious does store our past experiences and memories, good and bad, and that in itself can affect our birth experience. We have all heard, and people seem to love to tell, their 'nightmare' labor that lasted 5 days, or their emergency caesarean, or whatever it might be.

The first things you need to do in 'training' for a calm birth is:

1. Stop listening to any negative experiences related to birth. This will take strength! People will want to tell you, but honestly politely saying that if it wasn't a positive experience, I would really prefer to hear about it after my baby is born, is totally fine. You don't want that going into your 'bank' of memories before this experience. It will also be really important, with your partner, a doula perhaps, a close friend or confidante, to talk through your feelings about childbirth that you have likely built over many many years, from your parents, grandparents, from friends, even maybe sexual trauma or even just a fear of the unknown. These can be quite deep seated. It is important to acknowledge these and let them go. You can breathe them in and then let them go with an outbreath. You can

let them go even by throwing a stone into the river or the ocean or metaphorically throwing them away, or burning them written down on a piece of paper. This can be very cathartic and really is an important step in preparation for labour. By acknowledging fears/concerns and negative memories, they become less powerful.

We want to optimize the **good** pregnancy hormones that we talked about on page 14, primarily **oxytocin** in labor. Now, the 'autonomic nervous system' in our bodies, is a system of nerves that controls involuntary physiologic processes in our bodies-our heart rate, blood pressure, respiration, digestion and sexual arousal. Simply put, it is made up of the sympathetic and parasympathetic systems. Activating the *sympathetic nervous system* causes release of the hormone **adrenaline**, you're in 'flight and flight mode', a term you have probably encountered. This leads to an overall increase in activity, like 'survival' mode, heart rate goes up, as does your blood pressure, and the gastrointestinal tract stops working for a time. We all know that feeling when we have had a fright, or are just about to do something scary. That is the beginning of the unhelpful triad I mentioned earlier-the 'fear' beginning that fear-tension-pain cycle.

On the other hand, activation of the *parasympathetic nervous system* does not release adrenaline. It is often called the rest and digest state. It controls the body's ability to relax, which is what we need to access in labor. The heart rate is lower, the body is at rest and relaxed and it is in this state that we can produce the good pregnancy and labor hormone **oxytocin**. If we are in this state, blood can flow without constriction to the non-vital organs like the uterus, therefore causing less pain. If we were in fight or flight mode, blood would rush to our essential survival organs like the heart and lungs and in order to do this other blood vessels around the body will constrict, narrow, tighten, including those in the uterus. We want the blood to flow to the uterus, particularly during labor - the more blood flow to the uterus, the less pain during surges/contractions, and oxytocin flows, so here comes our second task in preparation for a calm birth. Also, scientific research has demonstrated that our brains wield significant control over how we perceive pain. The more relaxed a mother is, the more her body can naturally release endorphins-the body's natural pain relief.

2. We need to practice how to get into that calm state of relaxation so that we can access it when the time comes. This is where the 4/8 breath comes in, that I have been mentioning along the way.

We want to teach the conscious mind, with all that chatter, to switch off as much as possible so as to narrow your focus to the task ahead. So that you are in a state of deep relaxation and can enter that state quickly when the time comes. I really hope you might have been practising this already and you may even have found that it helps even in everyday life. This relaxed breath, where you inhale through your nose and exhale through your mouth for twice as long, the 4/8 breath I keep mentioning, will be the mainstay of your breathing in between contractions or surges. It is vitally important that with this breath you make sure your jaw is relaxed. The more relaxed you are in the jaw/vocal chord area, the more relaxed and open you are in your pelvic area.

MORE ON BREATHING TECHNIQUES

So I have talked about the **calm breath**, over and over again. And that is because there is literally no time like the present to start this practice. And maybe you already have. If you do yoga, you may know this as the yogi breath, and have been practising it for years. I was driving my daughter to a class the other day, and she could tell I was agitated. The whole atmosphere in the car was tense, we were late and I hate being late! But there was nothing we were going to be able to do about it, we were just going to be late, and it wasn't some make or break situation. It was a class. She suddenly pipes up at the traffic light, come on Mum, in through your nose for 4 and long out breath! I had led her the same way a few nights earlier when she was distressed about something. This is literally a breath for life!

The next important breath, that you again can practice, which you will use during your contractions or surges/ waves, whatever terminology you intend to use, is the **box**

breath. Here you can imagine working your way around a box-in for 4 through your nose, along the top of the box, then down the right side counting to 4 for the outbreath, (I like to go clockwise but you don't have to), then along the bottom in for 4 and then up the left side outbreath for 4. Some box breathing involves holding your breath, this does not, you must keep the free flow of oxygen. As labour progresses you can do 5 counts as you go round the box but don't do any more than that. Always 4 or 5. This will probably be enough for earlier contractions but you will likely have to pop round that box more than once when the surges/contractions start to lengthen. Just keep going around, visualizing the box, or you could even have a picture of it, until the surge has ended. Honestly the more you can stay in this zone through labour and particularly when you reach active labor, the better. And always keep your jaw relaxed. If noises come, welcome them, they will likely be low and animalistic, probably lower as your baby descends further. I was a very vocal labourer (is that a thing?), possibly because in my other life I'm a singer but I do know that the breathwork I had studied in singing for however many years helped no end in this process.

Lastly is the **welcome breath**. This sounds lovely doesn't it? It was certainly my favorite every time. This requires concentration and focus, but you will be in the right state for that if you have followed this breathwork all the way through your labor. This breath is going to culminate in you meeting your baby. This occurs right after a stage in labor called 'transition' and there will be more explanation about this later, but this breath comes when you are ready and your body feels the urge to push your baby out. For me, it was quite instinctive, your body knows what to do, enable it: take a full breath in, and then a long slow exhale through your mouth, with pursed lips, as you bear down. You are really directing this breath all the way down to your pelvis, where your cervix is open and ready. ALWAYS with jaw and neck relaxed. This maybe accompanied by a low sound, mine certainly was! And that is fine. But make sure you keep that breath coming, you will be breathing your baby out. Never, ever hold your breath to push, it will make you tense in your mouth/jaw/face area, which mimics how open or tense/closed you are down below where you are moving your baby through the birth canal.

RHYTHM

As a lifelong musician, I cannot leave this section without a mention of the power of rhythm in labor. Whether it is repeating a phrase or affirmation in a rhythmic way during contractions or moving or rocking in a rhythmic way during labor, these can be helpful in getting through a contraction or surge/wave. Many women will do this instinctively during labor and should be encouraged.

INVOLVE YOUR PARTNER

The more you can involve your partner in this practice, the better. As you enter the third trimester and the arrival of your baby is drawing nearer, being able to work together on training this relaxing breath, not only can calm your mind at the end of a long day or even to start one, it will give you both a shared space that your partner can help you access when the time comes. Having an object or signal or word that helps you get into that space is helpful to decide on together. This can be called an **anchor**. Something that will trigger that practice, and remind you of where you have been before, in that deeply relaxed state. The more you can use this breath during labor, the more you can keep adrenaline at bay and keep the blood and oxytocin flowing for labor to progress. Oxytocin flow is increased with deep breathing and meditation. It is important to be aware, in the coming weeks and in labor itself, that oxytocin, the hormone that initiates and then strengthens labor, is increased naturally by physical touch, hugging, holding hands, massage, cuddling and intimacy. These can be added to your toolbox for labor.

GUIDED MEDITATIONS/VISUALISATIONS

There are many many resources out there, particularly on youtube, listed under guided meditation for labour and delivery, active labor meditation, some are under hypnobirthing. I would spend some time with your partner going through some of these. Listen to the words they use and the music. Does this help to soothe you while doing your relaxed breath or are you finding something annoying? Be harsh, ideally you want to find one or two that work for you both while practicing your relaxing breath. This can also help you plan a labor play list, music that soothes, relaxes and connects you to each other.

A CALM ENVIRONMENT FOR A CALM BIRTH

We will be talking about birth plans later and we have already touched on birth place, but as part of our intention for a calm experience, wherever you labor and ultimately deliver your baby, you can make something of that environment, you can bring a personal touch, and your partner, again, is essential for this set up. You will be concentrating on your relaxing and box breathing but make sure your partner and you have the things packed or have the items at home to make the space and environment personalized. I wish I had had this advice when giving birth. My experiences were all in hospital, but I don't think I even thought about the idea of bringing in little lights or a favorite soft blanket or throw, some room spray or essential oils that I found helpful or soothing. You can do all of this, wherever you are having your baby, bringing a little bit of home comfort with you. It will also signal to those caring for you in hospital that your decisions and ideas are intentional.

PERINEAL MASSAGE

One technique you can look to do with your partner as you practice your breathing techniques in the weeks coming up to labor itself, is perineal massage. From around **34–35 weeks of pregnancy**—massaging the area between the vagina and anus—can help the tissues become more flexible and better prepared for stretching during birth. To do this, wash your hands, apply a little natural oil (like vitamin E, almond, or olive oil), and place your thumbs about one to two inches inside the vagina. Or your partner can do it for you. Press gently downwards and to the sides, creating a slow stretching motion until you feel mild tingling or pressure (but not pain). Do this for about 5–10 minutes, a few times a week.

Research shows that regular perineal massage **reduces the likelihood of perineal tears and the need for an episiotomy**, especially for **first-time mothers**. It can also increase confidence and body awareness going into labor.

CHECKLIST FOR CALM BIRTHING

In this chapter I have brought many things that we haven't talked about yet but this Chapter is **to refer back to during your preparation**. Start practising your breathwork as you enter this third trimester and start thinking about the atmosphere under which you want to welcome your baby into the world. You have control over this, you have power and intention, and your body was made to do this, never forget that.

1. Politely decline to listen to negative birth stories during pregnancy, and question your own ideas and thoughts around pregnancy, setting free and 'throwing out' or cleansing yourself of negative ideas around birth,

2. Breath work practice:

   - Calm Breath
   - Box Breathing
   - Welcome Breath

3. Find favourite meditations/visualisations to listen to during the third trimester to help you get into that relaxed state, or get back to it, if a turn of events has brought you out of it at some point in labor, which can happen.

4. Decide on your anchor with your partner-this could be a particular touch, an object, a piece of music, candlelight, a movement you make,

5. Don't forget the power of physical touch in labor, hugging, holding hands, cuddling, kissing, gentle physical affection,

6. Decide on one or more positive affirmations to use when needed

7. Decide what terms you want your care providers to use in front of you during your labor, for

instance for contractions you may want waves or surges

8. If there is any way of letting your HCP or hospital know your wishes ahead of time about the environment you are trying to create that can be helpful, and that they respect your wishes

9. Gather your labour room atmosphere tools and music choices

10. Perineal massage

11. ** Make sure to also read the section on **calm cesarean**, in the cesarean section in the next chapter so you know what to ask about, in case you end up needing a surgical birth .

Using these techniques and training for them can lead to a calmer, more empowered birth experience. It takes childbirth back to its natural state instead of a fear-inducing clinical event. These techniques challenge the fear-tension-pain cycle by encouraging expectant mothers to visualize their birthing process as a progression of natural, purposeful surges or waves (contractions), each one bringing them closer to their child. Lastly, the techniques mentioned here, any further reading or training you might do in hypnobirthing or deep relaxation, is the beginning of a lifelong legacy. It can inform your parenting and help you become the calm, confident parent you want to be.

REFLECTION EXERCISE: ENVISION YOUR IDEAL BIRTH EXPERIENCE

Take a quiet moment to envision your ideal birth experience. Having thought through and discussed with your partner the checklist above, now close your eyes and visualize the setting, sounds, and feelings you wish to surround you on that day. Consider how you want to feel—calm, empowered, supported—and what steps you might take to create this environment. Write down your thoughts and share them with your partner or support team to ensure everyone is aligned with your vision. This exercise can clarify your preferences and guide conversations with your healthcare provider as you prepare for the months ahead.

EMBRACING THE THIRD TRIMESTER

Definition: Beginning of week 28 to delivery

Excitement and anticipation is building, your baby is growing rapidly and becoming more 'present', with more pronounced movements. Your center of gravity will start to shift and as you move closer to delivery, your breathing may feel somewhat restricted, as your baby takes up more space, until the baby moves down or 'drops' further into the pelvis when you'll be able to breathe again but your bladder will feel like you want to go all the time, as by this time your baby is sitting right on your bladder!

I debated about this but, on balance, I think you need a visual here. Knowing even a small amount about your anatomy and how and where things lie in your body can only be helpful, to show how perfectly your body is designed for this process, and how during this remarkable few months, your body is preparing, setting the stage if you like, for your baby to be born. One very important piece of advice, which I mentioned briefly at the end of Chapter 3: I would advise against getting approximations of the baby weight. This is generally inaccurate and breeds fear. In my pregnancies in the UK, this was NEVER discussed, even if the doctor/midwife might do a calculation. Babies and women are designed to be born vaginally. It is not always possible, of course, and positioning can be troublesome but the bones in the pelvis actually move and the baby turns, in order for this process to work. Trust it!

I will not be mentioning an approximate weight for each month, after 31 weeks and 3lb, as this is not helpful information. We all know our 'baby weight' and that of our friends and family. You are entering a rapid time of growth!! My first came in at 8 lb, and then I had two girls over 9 pounds. But I had no idea what weight they would be, I just knew it would be a healthy weight from the measuring of the fundal height at my appointments. Again, our bodies are designed for this. And also remember that your baby is designed for this too-the skull bones are not hard like ours are when our babies are born, they are soft and malleable at this stage, for a reason, and will overlap as the pelvis widens. I had no idea what weight they would come in at and have found, anecdotally, that those predictions are way more often than not, inaccurate, sometimes wildly. I'm glad I didn't know any predictions. I was preparing to birth my baby, not some number of pounds or kilos! Research actually does show that weight predictions can be up to

15% inaccurate, often over-estimating rather than under-estimating weight.

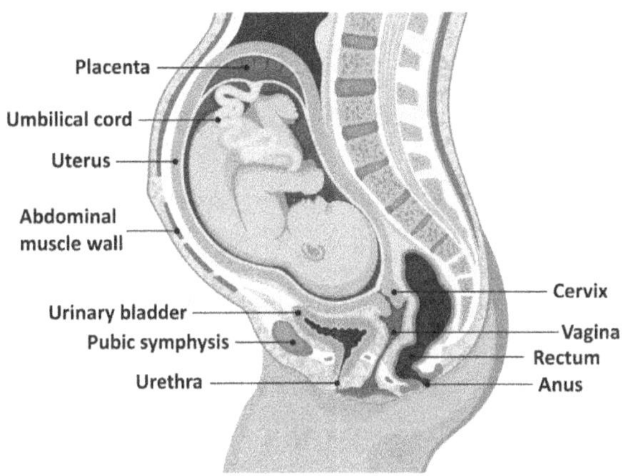

FACTS FIRST

Week 28: Your baby is probably about 15 inches long at this point, hiccuping, breathing well (although lungs not fully mature yet) blinking and sleeping. To give you some context for this trimester, your baby will at least double in size during this time; this is an intense period of growth, particularly fat accumulation under the skin, once the important embryological development has occurred and everything is in place.

Week 29: Up at 16 inches long now. Fat accumulation continues, baby's brain continues to grow and can perform more functions.

Week 30: Temperature regulation is now controlled by your baby's brain and they start to lose the lanugo hair on their bodies.

Week 31: Your baby has now reached about 3 pounds. More brain development and connections being made-your baby is using all five senses, and sleeping quite a bit!

Week 32: As I already mentioned, lanugo hair is disappearing and the fat accumulation means that your baby's skin is not transparent any more. Also size wise, think melon, cantaloupe.

Week 33: More growth and probably some intense kicks coming in as your baby gains strength, practising for life outside the womb.

Week 34: Your baby is now 17/18 inches long. If you are carrying a boy, the testes (balls) will start to make their way down to the scrotum this week.

Week 35: Growth continues, including brain growth and development. This is the point at which your baby's head will be settling, we hope, head down, but not all babies behave exactly as we predict....

your HCP will keep an eye on this and discuss options if baby's position is not head down (ie breech-more on this later).

Week 36: All systems are ready to go and more growth takes place.

Week 37-40: Your baby is now 'full term' and fully formed and ready for life outside the womb. Your baby will now signal its arrival anytime between now and 42 weeks. Each mother and baby has their own personal gestation. It, of course, can be more uncomfortable as your baby continues to grow and move inside you, but I do believe that each mother and baby has its time, so be patient and enjoy the togetherness, despite the discomfort, it is an incredibly special time.

IN THIS CHAPTER WE WILL DISCUSS:

- Your appointments
- What to prepare during this trimester
- Third trimester symptoms and comfort measures
- Your birth plan
- Considering a doula
- Packing your hospital bag
- Signs of labor
- Practising calm birthing techniques

YOUR APPOINTMENTS IN THE THIRD TRIMESTER

Your appointments will continue to include a check of your urine, and blood pressure, fetal heart rate check, the fundal height measurement (remember the number of cm equals the approximate number of weeks of pregnancy), checking for any swelling in the feet or hands, baby position (more from weeks 34/35 as baby starts to settle), blood test for anemia if needed, glucose screening test, if this hasn't already been done, and, of course, any symptoms that need discussion. Depending on your country, as mentioned in Vaccines Chapter 1, you may be offered the TDap vaccine, early in the 3rd trimester, (to protect against pertussis also known as whooping cough, diphtheria and tetanus.) Once you've had this vaccine, the antibodies you produce will be passed to your baby through the placenta and can help protect them before they are old enough to be vaccinated themselves, which does not start until they are 2 months old. Your visits will likely increase in frequency as you get closer to your due date. You will be tested for Group B strep likely around 36 weeks.

Group B Strep explained: this is a bacteria which can be found in the vagina asymptomatically (so you don't have symptoms and would not know it is there). This can be present in about a quarter to a third of healthy women with no consequence. However, when you're pregnant, and positive for this bacteria ('GBS positive'), there is a small chance that your baby can pick up a Group B strep infection as they move through the birth canal (a risk of about one baby per 200 babies-this is only in mothers who test positive). This can be a potentially serious infection, so in order to prevent this possibility, women who are GBS positive are offered intravenous (through the vein) antibiotics during labor, to protect your baby from any likely infection, which reduces the risk to one in 4000. In a woman who tests negative for the bacteria, the risk of this infection in the baby is one in 5000.

There are some risk factors that increase the chances of a baby developing the infection such as:

- Prolonged rupture of membranes (that is when your water breaks quite a long time before you deliver your baby, 18 hours+),
- Your baby is premature
- Mothers with fever during labor
- GBS found on testing during labor vaginally or in the urine
- Previous GBS-affected baby.

The infection in babies usually occurs within the first couple of days after delivery and can include meningitis, pneumonia or sepsis, but again, this is thankfully a rare occurrence.

Different HCP and countries tackle this issue differently. In the USA, insurance generally covers GBS testing around 36/37 weeks and women are offered prophylactic antibiotics (to prevent the illness in their babies) during labor. In the UK, because studies have shown that many of the testing is inaccurate and that the bacteria can come and go in the vagina, and that previous screening for many years did not show a decrease in the number of babies who develop GBS, they use a risk based approach, meaning they identify women who are most at risk (using the criteria above). These women are then treated with the IV antibiotics during labor.

THE THIRD TRIMESTER CHECKLIST: WHAT TO PREPARE

Reaching the third trimester really brings into focus many of those final details that need preparation and thought. Think about and ultimately finalize any childcare arrangements you might need for any little ones you have. Whether it's coordinating with family or securing a babysitter or daycare, having this sorted gives you peace of mind. And can also bring into your mind support and how you want that network to look as you bring your baby home. Don't forget to organize important documents for the hospital too. Keep your health insurance details (US), birth plan, and contact numbers in one easy-to-access folder. My nesting instinct in the third trimester really kicked in, and with it quite a bit of energy, to plan, even though I was also working at the time. Assembling the crib is a fun one to do with your partner (maybe...). Baby-proofing cupboards and outlets maybe worth doing now as the crawling phase can come quicker than you think, amongst sleepless nights and breastfeeding…. there's nothing like creating that safe space for your baby for focussing the mind, and if you have a dedicated room/nursery for your baby you can have fun decorating it. Something to think about-I already told you about the yard sale I had just before finding out I was pregnant with my third…the point is, there is not much you actually NEED. A crib yes, a beautiful matching changing unit and other furniture to go with, not so much. You could save some of that for other things like your diaper/nappy fund! Make sure you have your car seat and a changing pouch, stroller and possibly a baby wearing device as long as your back is up to it, or one your partner is happy to wear.

In the US, review your insurance policies to make sure they cover all maternity and pediatric needs. Updating or creating a will, and estate planning ensures your child's future is protected, even in unforeseen circumstances. These tasks might feel overwhelming, but they're important steps in being prepared. Discuss these with your partner to have everything aligned before the baby arrives. Believe me, these things are easier to organise before you have babies in your life!

Practical household arrangements are equally important. Stock up on essentials like toilet paper and cleaning supplies. If you have time, freeze meals ahead of time—one-pot dishes or casseroles work well and free you up during those early postpartum days when cooking is the last thing on your mind. A full pantry and ready-to-eat meals are invaluable once your hands are full with a newborn.

Emotionally preparing for labor and parenthood is vital. Make sure to read and re-read the Bonus Chapter 4-practising these techniques and identifying a few guided meditations from youtube that you enjoy, is also very helpful, if you are planning the natural route. Identifying and attending birthing classes is important preparation. I would go as far as to call this an essential component of your pre-delivery third trimester plan. The hospital you are planning to deliver at may have classes, or there are many advertised online. If there is any way you can attend in person this is preferable. Doing classes in your area may mean that you meet other women who are giving birth at a similar time to you. You won't maybe realize this now but meeting couples who are going through the same thing as you can be incredibly powerful. I have already mentioned that In the UK, I was able to sign up for classes with the National Childbirth Trust, where women are matched in classes with those giving birth in the same 6 week period. The 7 other women I met in that class, back in 2004, remain dear friends of mine, and although we are now based on three continents, we stay in touch and meet whenever we can. These classes should include labor positions. Practising these with your partner can make a world of difference when the time comes. It's important to have options. Third trimester is training time!

Making sure to involve your partner in all these practices is essential to strengthen the teamwork necessary for the event. Practicing massage techniques and comfort measures together not only foster connection but also ensures they know how best to support you when labor kicks in.

Think about relaxation aids you might want to take to the hospital with you or have ready at home for home births. From personal experience I would definitely recommend a birth ball (I recommend the 45cm as a good size) or a peanut ball. These items can be game-changers in making your birthing environment more manageable. The birthing ball is also great for rhythmic movement. I have added a list of birth positions and a visual at the back of the book, make sure to practice these and write down your favorites on your toolkit list.

YOUR BODY IN THE THIRD TRIMESTER AND ALLEVIATING COMMON DISCOMFORTS

Looking back at the second trimester list on page 71, these symptoms are not going to miraculously disappear. These may well continue, but accompanied by a few more.

Possibly leaky breasts: as your body prepares for birth, you can, but not always, develop leakage of yellow colored fluid from your breasts. This is colostrum, it's nothing to worry about. The yellow fluid is the 'prebreast' milk fluid which you produce the first few days after your baby is born, rich in antibodies and protein. When the milk comes in (around day 5, more on this in Chapter 7) it looks more like milk! With more fat and milk sugar as well as the protein.

Spotting after sex: this can happen, as the cervix is more sensitive at this time, but it is not a sign of labor starting. If you have a pinky/brownish mucus discharge accompanied by contractions or surges, that could be a sign that labor is starting. If you have persistent or bright red blood, call your HCP.

Increased movements: your baby is getting up there in size now, and movements will feel more powerful. You can check movements, preferably at the same time every day, and see roughly how long it takes to get to 10 kicks or even flutters. You should get to 10 movements in 2 hours. You don't need to do this every day but if things seem quieter or you're worried, then choose a time when your baby is usually more active, and count kicks, rolls, flutters, they all count. If there is a noticeable change or you are not reaching 10 movements in 2 hours, then make sure to contact your HCP immediately.

Increasing shortness of breath: Your baby and the expanding uterus are taking up a lot of room now, and the lungs start to feel the effects of literally not having the space to expand fully, as you get into your final month of pregnancy.

Difficulty sleeping: I know I mentioned this one in Chapter 3 but just re-iterating. Your sleep may become particularly difficult in that last month due to the size of the baby. Make sure you are lying propped up on pillows from that final month or on your side. A pillow between your knees can also help with comfort in this position. You can also experience quite vivid and strange dreams at this stage in the pregnancy. They can be quite fantastical. This can be related to your hormones but also your subconscious processing all the conflicting thoughts and anxieties about pregnancy and childbirth.

Sharp shooting pain in pelvis: curious but common symptom. A sudden sharp pain deep in the pelvis, sometimes in the US called 'lightning crotch'. It can almost feel like an electric shock. The cause is not known but it could be the baby pressing on a nerve in the cervix. It is not a sign that labor is starting. Try changing positions and it should settle quickly.

Back pain and pelvic pressure: your baby is descending and the pelvis is gradually widening so it is quite common to feel more pelvic pressure. Keep an eye on your posture-it is common to lean back at this stage but this will really strain the muscles in your back. Here are a few tips to ease back pain:

- Try to stand as straight and tall as possible, chest out and shoulders back and relaxed, knees slightly bent, don't lock them,
- If you have to stand for periods of time, use a wide stance and try to get off your feet every 1-2 hours,
- Lying on your side with a pillow between your legs, with knees a little bent, will help to relieve back pain,
- When sitting, use a pillow behind you to keep your back as straight as possible, and have your knees at right angles
- Try to wear flat shoes with good arch support
- Some people are helped by a pregnancy support belt (I actually used one quite a bit, having a scoliosis already, I was already troubled with back pain at times. The evidence for these is

patchy but I would give it a try if your back pain is bothering you,

- If you have to lift things, use a wide stance when squatting down to retrieve item, and keep your back straight and use your leg strength to lift, but know your limitations,

- Heat or cold pads and massage can give some relief,

- Stay **active** as much as you can. And this advice takes you right through until your baby is born. Engaging in low-impact exercise at this stage is so helpful-walking or swimming is great.

- Best not to lie flat at this stage, certainly as you get closer to your due date, the increasing weight of the uterus and your baby will be pressing down on the main artery and vein in your body (aorta and vena cava) and it is best avoided from about 28 weeks. Lie on your side or propped up with pillows if you prefer to be on your back, just not flat on your back.

You can consider alternative therapies like prenatal massage or acupuncture to alleviate discomfort. These can help relieve tension, enhance circulation, and manage stress. Prenatal massages ease sore muscles uniquely for pregnancy, while acupuncture targets points to promote relaxation and balance.

As I mentioned above, maintaining a healthy lifestyle is pivotal in minimizing these discomforts. Staying active with low-impact exercises like swimming or prenatal yoga keeps your muscles toned and flexible without excessive strain. The buoyancy of water in swimming alleviates joint pressure while offering cardiovascular benefits. Ensuring adequate hydration supports your body's increased blood volume and helps flush out toxins. Balancing nutrition with wholesome foods like lean proteins, fruits, and vegetables nourishes both you and your baby.

Remember, you're not alone in this final phase of pregnancy. Many women experience similar challenges, and reaching out for support can make all the difference. Noting down experiences and symptoms (in the notes section at the back of the book) and engaging in conversations with your healthcare provider, ensures you're making informed choices about treatments and lifestyle adjustments.

Try to focus on what works best for you and your unique experience. Each pregnancy is different, so what brings relief to one person might not work for another. Stay open to trying new methods and techniques to find what brings you the most comfort.

THINKING ABOUT YOUR WISHES FOR YOUR BIRTH AND WRITING YOUR PLAN

As your due date approaches, thinking about your birth wishes feels empowering. We plan for pretty much every important event in our lives, whether that is your wedding or graduation celebrations or other important life events and so planning for this is no different. But, this is very important: It's less about scripting every detail and more about understanding and communicating what matters most to you. Consider what kind of environment you want. Do you envision a calm, dimly lit space or a bustling room filled with support? Picture who you want by your side, guiding and coaching you on. Maybe it's just your partner or perhaps a close friend or family member too. Maybe a doula. Envision the comfort measures that suit you—warm compresses, soothing music, or aromatherapy.

While it's tempting to call it a "plan," I like the idea of "wishes." Plans can suggest rigidity, but birth is unpredictable. Wishes grant flexibility, allowing room for the unexpected while focusing on what's meaningful to you. It's about the journey, not just the destination. Discuss these wishes with your healthcare provider and partner. Their support in understanding and respecting your preferences will provide reassurance, even if things don't unfold exactly as you imagined.

Think about pain management options. Are you leaning toward an unmedicated birth, or are you open to using medication if needed? Understanding your preferences and the options at your chosen place of delivery helps your healthcare team provide the best care aligned with your and your partners wishes. If you're considering an epidural, discuss when you'd like one, any concerns you have, and how that might look for your labor.

Consider also how involved you want your partner to be during labor. Would you like them to help with breathing exercises or be there for emotional support? Discuss these roles beforehand to ensure everyone is prepared. This shared understanding fosters a supportive environment where everyone feels engaged and valued.

Reflect on what postpartum care looks like for you. Do you want delayed cord-clamping? Do you prefer immediate skin-to-skin contact with your baby, or do you want some initial quiet time to recover? These decisions can shape your early bonding experiences and lay the foundation for parenthood.

Keep in mind that flexibility is key. Birth can be unpredictable, and sometimes interventions are necessary for the safety of you and your baby. Stay open to adjustments and trust that your healthcare team has your best interests at heart. Your wishes guide the experience, but adaptability ensures a positive outcome.

Remember, this process isn't about achieving perfection, but rather about creating a nurturing environment where you feel empowered and supported. It's about advocating for yourself and trusting your body's ability to bring new life into the world.

Remember birth plans come in all shapes and sizes depending on you and your partner. It can be a thorough document or could be some notes jotted down in the back of this book. Just make sure you keep them handy for the big day so that your birth support/s are aware of them and they can relay to your HCP, and be advocates in that room for you.

Things to include in your Birth Wishes/Birth Plan:

- Start with some **basic details** about you and your partner
- **Location preferences:** where you ideally want to give birth-home, birthing center, hospital
- **Support team:** companions including during assisted delivery/Caesarean-partner, doula, family
- Whether you would be comfortable if **training** midwives/nurses or doctors to be present
- What **terminology** do you want used during labor
- What kind of **environment**/lighting do you want for your labor room
- **Labor preferences:** including keeping active during labor, birthing equipment you intend

to use, including birthing balls, birthing pools, positions for laboring

- **Monitoring** and **examination** preferences in labor
- **Pain management:** outline what your preferences are for pain relief, natural and drugs
- **Positions** for birth
- **Intervention stance:** including induction, episiotomy, assisted delivery, Caesarean
- **Postpartum wishes:** including immediate bonding time, delayed cord clamping, delivery of placenta, including drug assisted (syntometrine)
- **Feeding** preferences for your baby
- **Vitamin K** for baby after birth
- **Eye drops** for baby after birth

Don't worry about some of these terms-all is explained in the next chapter on labor and delivery-you can note down questions you have in the back of the book, as you start to make your plan.

It is interesting to note that the sample birth plan supplied by the American College of Obstetricians and Gynecologists (ACOG) is a two page document whereas the one supplied by the National Health Service in the UK stretches to 11 pages, admittedly with much space to write your own thoughts but with some stark differences to the US one. The most significant one being what they call in the USA 'anaesthesia' options, meaning pain relief measures. It's a yes, no, not sure situation, about **epidurals** only.

In the UK however, 8 options are noted, including breathing and relaxation, massage, water, TENS machines, 'gas and air', pain relieving injections, and lastly epidurals. More on this in the next chapter but I would urge you to think about this when you are choosing where to give birth in the US-some hospitals may offer alternatives, and having options is what you want as you really don't know exactly how you're going to feel. Following the relaxation techniques and practicing them will go a long way to reducing fear and therefore pain. I can't stress this enough, they cause a reduction in pain for the reasons I mentioned before-blood flow to the uterus is better, therefore reducing pain on contractions/surges/waves.

I also found the terminology difference fascinating. In the UK plan they talk about 'analgesia', meaning pain relief, the definition of this word being 'absence of pain'. In the US document from the ACOG, they refer to ANAESTHESIA in the area of the birth plan regarding pain. This is revealing in itself. This means insensitivity to pain or 'controlled, temporary loss of sensitivity or awareness of pain that is induced for medical purposes'. It is putting the whole process in a 'medical' context, whereas we know it is a natural physiological process where you may need some pain relief support. A lot of food for thought there as you decide on your birth location, interventions and wishes.

THINKING ABOUT DELIVERY: CONSIDERING DOULA SUPPORT

It was issues like the one I highlighted above, about pain relief, that propelled me to train as a birth doula/advocate. The structure and establishment, particularly in the USA, is rather stacked against natural birth and the truth that birth is a physiological rather than a pathological process. And I wanted to be there to help women experience the kind of birth that they wanted, to own it, whatever that may be, in the context of their family, any past experiences or trauma, as a shared experience with their partner or special people, and to create something beautiful and memorable with the resources they and their team could bring to this incredible process. And to clarify, whatever kind of pain relief you and your partner decide is totally your decision, I just want to make sure you have options and know what to ask for.

Doulas can significantly impact labor, offering continuous emotional, physical support and advocacy of your and your partner's wishes. Make sure to interview potential doulas to discuss their experience and approach. Ask about their philosophy on childbirth and how they handle unexpected situations. Discuss your expectations and roles to ensure they understand what you need. A doula should feel like a natural extension of your support team, bringing comfort and confidence.

We become your anchor. We focus on your well-being, helping you stay calm and centered. During labor, emotions can run high, and having a doula ensures you have someone advocating for your wishes and preferences. We ensure your birth plan is followed as much as possible. Our expertise in comfort measures like breathing techniques, massage, rebozo work and positioning can make labor more manageable. We can help manage other family members and give your partner specific roles in the process so they also feel valued and essential.

Collaboration between doulas and healthcare teams is crucial for a cohesive birthing experience. Doulas act as bridges, facilitating communication with healthcare providers to ensure everyone is on the same page. They can clarify medical jargon, helping you make informed decisions without feeling overwhelmed. While medical staff focus on clinical aspects, doulas prioritize your comfort and preferences. They adapt to changes in the birth plan, ensuring it reflects your evolving needs. Their presence complements medical care, offering holistic support.

The benefits of having a doula extend beyond emotional support. Studies show that doulas can:

- significantly reduce the need for pain measures,
- can help reduce the length of labor
- decrease the need for medical interventions like induction with pitocin, forceps deliveries and cesarean sections.

- enhanced satisfaction with the birthing experience, feeling more in control and empowered.

PACKING YOUR HOSPITAL BAG: ESSENTIALS FOR LABOR DAY

Getting ready for the big day involves more than just mental preparation. It's all about ensuring you have everything you need when the time comes. Start with comfy clothing. Loose, breathable outfits will be essential during and after labor. A nightshirt is perfect for giving birth in. NB: If a hospital asks you to put on a hospital gown, just politely say you have your own clothes for labor. If they seem to insist, as for written policy. The questions should go away. And in fact, if you are unsure about other protocols, that is always a good answer. As for written policy. A few changes of clothes are handy, along with a cozy robe and slippers. Don't forget toiletries—think toothbrush, hairbrush, and your favorite shampoo. Consider including a favorite oil or lotion for your skin. These small comforts can make a significant difference during your birth center or hospital stay. You will also need to gather items for your baby: include soft clothing like bodysuits and hats. A warm blanket is essential for swaddling your little one, offering them comfort in their new world. There's also the car seat, crucial for bringing your beautiful baby home safely. Remember to set it up in advance and know how to fix it in the car, to avoid last-minute stress.

For breastfeeding, pack essentials like a feeding bra and breast pads. Important documents such as your ID, insurance information, and birth plan are vital too. Keep them in an easily accessible folder so you can quickly grab them when needed.

Items for comfort and relaxation are essential to maintain the calm we talked about in Chapter 4. Aromatherapy oils or lotions. And also make sure to have that cosy blanket that helps to take you into one of your guided meditations, and any other anchor you and your partner have been using as you prepare with breathing techniques, a smooth stone or even a soft toy. Also remember to bring a speaker to play your music. Don't forget snacks, drinks and your water bottle.

Your partner's essentials matter as well. They'll need snacks also, and drinks to stay energized; labor can be long, and they'll want to be at their best to support you. A change of clothes and toiletries ensures they're comfortable too. Being prepared allows them to focus on what's most important: being there for you.

Unexpected scenarios do happen, so consider packing extra items. An extended hospital stay means needing additional clothing and personal items. Books, magazines, or puzzles can provide a welcome distraction during downtime.

Preparation gives you peace of mind, knowing you're ready for whatever comes your way. As you pack this bag of essentials, think of it as curating a little slice of home. Each item contributes to making the experience as comforting and smooth as possible for both you and your partner.

Make sure that you pack any items you want to use to make the room more comfortable or atmospheric for you, even battery operated tea lights or certain smells/aromatherapy oils that help create a serene and tranquil atmosphere in your birthing space wherever that may be. It is your partner who needs to know where these are and how you want them used.

I've placed the Hospital Bag packing list in the back (on page 251) to check off when the time comes.

RECOGNIZING LABOR SIGNS: WHAT TO WATCH FOR

I have heard many stories, particularly in the USA, of people being in labor for 5 days or very long periods of time. Actual 'active labor' will never be as long as this and it is a lot about terminology. I mentioned in Chapter 4 about not listening to negative labor stories, and the stories where people talk about labor lasting for days are really not helpful to you right now. I am going to explain some important facts about this terminology and how to know when you are in labor for real.

There are a number of signs that suggest **labor is likely to be approaching** but it could still be sometime before you get into active or established labor:

- The loss of your mucus plug. You may pass some mucus mixed with some bloody streaks, which is the protective barrier at the cervix. This is a sign the cervix is beginning to soften, thin and ultimately open. (This can happen weeks before labor actually starts though).

- 'Random contractions' or surges, these can be the beginning of labor and are worth paying attention to. They will be uncomfortable, possibly painful (depending on your pain threshold and also your level of relaxation and calm) but not so much that you can't continue with what you are doing. They are random if you time them. It is important to welcome these early surges/contractions and not resist them. Also, try to rest when you can as this heralds some exciting and active time ahead! This is the very beginning of you being able to meet your baby! (In the US this is often termed prodromal labor or 'early' labor). The contractions can be strong but they are not consistent and don't progress, meaning they don't get stronger and closer together and start lasting longer, so this is not labor and therefore 'prodromal or early **labor**' is a very confusing term. Some call it false labor which I also don't like. There is nothing false about this-some women do have random quite uncomfortable contractions for quite some time leading up to labor establishing for real. And it can be exhausting. Pre-labor is probably a better term. It is really important to rest as much as you can between these contractions,, hydrate and maybe even have a bath at some point.

NOTE: This is NOT the same as Braxton Hicks contractions: these are random **painless (or mildly uncomfortable)** contractions-where you feel a tightening across your belly. They can last varying amounts of time. They can come as early as 16-20 weeks (but more common from 3rd trimester) and are totally normal. Often brought on by activity, dehydration, exhaustion, sex, a full bladder, or when you are tired. Not everyone has them. The important thing to know is, this is NOT labour either. This is your body gearing up, practising if you like, for when labor starts proper. I found them quite exciting, and had more with each pregnancy. The important thing to note is that these are *painless and normal*. They can feel a little uncomfortable at times but they are just preparing your uterus.

- Water breaking-note the date and time of this and roughly the amount. Don't panic! Is there any color or odor?-important questions that

> your HCP will ask you when you let them know
> this has happened.
> - New low back ache-this can be a constant low
>   ache or comes in waves.
> - vomiting/diarrhoea

It is important to note that ACTIVE labor contractions/ surges have two important distinctions from anything you may have felt before. ACTIVE Labor is when:

1. Surges or contractions occur at **regular** intervals, ie 5 minutes apart etc. AND
2. They grow longer and stronger over time AND
3. Gradually get closer together

Pay attention to other changes like increased vaginal discharge or spotting. A "bloody show" is common as your cervix continues to dilate and soften/thin, preparing for birth. It is like a more bloody version of the mucus plug. This can be a sign that labor is imminent, especially if paired with other signs. It is different to the mucus plug as it is always bloody, whereas a mucus plug only may have the odd streak of blood.

Trust your instincts; you know your body best. If you feel something's happening, don't hesitate to contact your healthcare provider. They can offer guidance on whether it's time to make your way to the hospital or birthing center.

Remember, each woman's labor is unique. Some experience all signs, while others may have only a few. The key is staying calm and prepared for when labor begins in earnest. The fact is labor is not a sprint, it's more of a marathon. At this point you can start to access the tools you have been practising, the equipment you think will be useful, the music you want to play etc and start along the road. You can think of your tools/methods at points along the road or mile markers where you feel like you might need to choose a new tool/change positions/shake things up and then you get to the next marker and use a different technique on your journey. I have made a list of possible tools in the back of the book-you can make your own list taking ideas from this list and adding any of your own personal ones. But at the root of all is your breath, the most powerful tool you own.

You don't need to panic, there is most likely plenty of time to be at home in early labor, with all your home comforts and familiarity which will help you access that relaxed place we talked about in Chapter 4. Your body knows what it's doing, and soon enough, you'll be holding your baby in your arms. More on when to go to your birthing place in the next chapter!

REMINDER TO TURN BACK TO CHAPTER 4: KEEP PRACTICING THOSE CALM TECHNIQUES: PREPARING FOR LABOR

In this last week or so when you may experience more signs that your baby is arriving imminently, it is important to keep practising your relaxation techniques for labor, to make sure that oxytocin flows when the time for birthing your baby arrives.

These methods aren't just tools; they're lifelines during one of life's most intense moments:

- Remember your **calm breath**. Inhale deeply through your nose for 4, then exhale slowly for 8. You can even start with 4/4, and gradually work towards 4/8. This not only calms the mind but helps manage pain.
- **Guided meditations** will be spoken relaxations that can guide you into a deeply calm, relaxed state. During these you want to be focussing on your breathing, releasing tension and relaxing your muscles. These can include positive affirmations. It is good to have a few positive affirmations written down that you can refer to in labor.
- Make sure you have chosen at least **1-2 visualizations** on youtube. These will include mental images or scenarios that can help during labor, even the image of a flower opening to

represent the cervix itself opening, or waves on a beach that can represent labor unfolding.

Involving your partner in practicing these techniques can make a big difference. Partner-led breathing exercises can deepen your connection and create a shared rhythm. Practice massage techniques together; gentle back or foot massages can be soothing during labor, offering comfort and relief. These activities foster teamwork, allowing your partner to be an active participant in your birthing experience, not just a bystander. Review positions for your tool kit.

Practice, practice, practice! I can't emphasize this enough.

Remember, these techniques aren't just for labor; practicing them beforehand ensures you're ready when the time comes. Like any skill, familiarity breeds confidence. When surges/contractions start, you'll find solace in these well-practiced methods. They become second nature, guiding you through each phase.

As we conclude this chapter, remember that preparation isn't about control; it's about empowerment. These techniques and practices equip you with the ability to enter labor with confidence, calmness and without fear. Embrace them as part of your birthing toolkit, knowing they will support you in every moment of labor's intensity.

Onward to meeting your baby!

Chapter 5 Checklist:

THE BIG PICTURE

- Baby's movements are stronger and more "present"; your center of gravity shifts.
- Shortness of breath is common until baby "drops," after which bladder pressure increases.
- Avoid fixating on estimated fetal weight—measurements are often off and can create unnecessary worry.

BABY'S GROWTH (HIGHLIGHTS)

- Weeks 28–34: rapid brain development; fat stores build; lanugo recedes; stronger kicks.
- ~Week 35+: baby ideally settles **head-down** (position checked at visits).
- Weeks 37–42: **term**; each mother–baby pair has their own timing.

APPOINTMENTS & ROUTINE CARE

- Ongoing checks: **blood pressure, urine, fetal heart, fundal height, swelling, symptoms, baby position.**
- Vaccines (per country guidance): **Tdap** in early third trimester to protect baby from pertussis.

- Labs as indicated: anemia check, glucose screening (if not done), others based on history.
- **Group B Strep (GBS)** around 36–37 weeks:

  - USA: universal screening; IV antibiotics in labor if positive.
  - UK: risk-based approach; antibiotics if risk factors/positive result.

THIRD TRIMESTER CHECKLIST (PRACTICAL PREP)

- **Home & logistics:** child care plans, car seat installed, essentials stocked, a few freezer meals.
- **Paperwork:** insurance details, birth wishes, key contacts in one folder.
- **Classes & community:** childbirth education; practice positions, massage, and comfort measures with your partner.
- **Tools that helps:** birth/peanut ball, speaker, simple relaxation anchors (oils, eye mask, cozy blanket).

COMMON SYMPTOMS & COMFORT TIPS

- **Breathlessness:** rest upright; side-lie with pillows; gentle walks.
- **Sleep trouble:** side-lying with knee pillow; short pre-bed stretch; screen wind-down.

- **Back/pelvic pressure:** posture check, hip squeezes, heat/cold, support belt (if helpful), swimming/walking.
- **"Lightning crotch":** brief positional changes usually help.
- **Heartburn/constipation:** small frequent meals; fluids between meals; fiber + fluids.
- **Colostrum leakage:** normal; use breast pads.
- **After sex spotting:** can be cervical sensitivity; persistent/bright red bleeding → call your HCP.

YOUR BIRTH WISHES (FLEXIBLE "PLAN")

- Focus on **what matters most** (environment, language, mobility, monitoring, positions, water use).
- Pain support spectrum: breathing/relaxation, water/TENS/massage, nitrous/meds, epidural—know your options.
- Post-birth preferences: **delayed cord clamping**, immediate **skin-to-skin**, newborn meds (vitamin K, eye prophylaxis), feeding plans.
- Share wishes with your partner and provider; keep expectations **flexible**.

CONSIDERING A DOULA

- Continuous support can shorten labor, reduce interventions, and improve satisfaction.

- Interview for fit: philosophy, teamwork with clinical staff, experience with unexpected changes.

HOSPITAL/BIRTH-BAG ESSENTIALS

- Comfortable labor outfit/robe, toiletries, lip balm, hair ties.
- Relaxation aids: playlist/speaker, oils/lotion, eye mask, focal item.
- Snacks/fluids for you and partner; chargers; copies of birth wishes; ID/insurance.
- Baby items: onesies/hat/blanket; car seat installed.
- Partner items

RECOGNIZING LABOR

- **Pre-labor signs:** mucus plug/bloody show, irregular tightenings, backache, GI upset, "water breaking."
- **Active labor looks like:** contractions that become **regular**, **longer/stronger**, and **closer together** over time.
- Braxton Hicks = usually painless/irregular "practice" tightenings.

WHEN TO CONTACT YOUR PROVIDER

- Decreased fetal movement after you've been feeling regular movements.
- Vaginal bleeding (more than light spotting) or **green/brown** fluid with water breaking.
- Fever, severe or persistent headache, visual changes, sudden facial/hand swelling, right-upper-abdominal pain.
- Regular, intensifying contractions; or your waters break (note **time, color, odor, amount**).

CALM TECHNIQUES: KEEP PRACTICING

- Daily **4/8 breathing**, guided meditations, and **chosen visualizations**.
- Partner practice: timing breaths, massage/hip squeezes, position changes.
- Think in "mile markers": rotate tools/positions as labor unfolds.

Bottom line: Prepare what you can, keep your circle supportive, stay flexible, and return to your breath. Your body and baby are designed for this. Make sure to have your labor toolkit list printed.

THE LABOR AND DELIVERY EXPERIENCE

OVERCOMING FEAR: BUILDING CONFIDENCE FOR DELIVERY DAY

As delivery day approaches, a mix of excitement and apprehension is completely normal. The unknown can stir up a whirlwind of emotions. Remember, if you've had time to prep, even a little, with calm birthing techniques then really, that's a huge step in the right direction. Knowledge is power, and understanding what to expect can transform fear into confidence. Labor isn't a one-size-fits-all experience. Each birth story is unique, but within this unpredictability lies a fundamental truth: your body knows how to nurture and bring forth this new life. Whatever your birth looks like in the end, having a positive experience with good communication and understanding, will have a profound effect on you in the weeks and even years ahead. I was talking to a friend the other day and 10 years on she still regrets something that happened in her labor, because she felt it could have been avoided had the people looking after her explained exactly where she was in her labor at that time.

Focus on what you can control—your mindset and preparation. Picture yourself in a serene space, surrounded by supportive people. Repeat affirmations that ground you: "I am strong," "My body is capable," or "Each surge/ wave brings me closer to meeting my baby." "I can do it/ this" "I am strong and powerful", "I am a brave woman". These simple statements can become powerful mantras that anchor your thoughts in confidence rather than fear. If you do have a special phrase or affirmation like this, or several, they can become an important part of your toolkit for labor. Saying a mantra like this rhythmically through your labor can be an incredibly powerful tool. I have added 'a list of affirmations' to your hospital bag list to remember to bring. Make sure they speak to you personally if you are using these.

Dig into the information you've gathered about labor. Read the stages and what each entails, and how miraculous our bodies are at preparing us for this. Your surges/waves/ contractions are not just random waves of discomfort; they're progress markers, showing you that your body is working effectively. Understanding this can transform apprehension into anticipation of what comes next. And you have your tools for each marker. Change them up as you progress. Reframe the sensations as productive and purposeful. And remember, the more you can remain in that calm state with your breathing, your rhythmic affirmations, your music, your visualisations, the more the oxytocin will flow, the blood vessels supplying the uterus will be open (and dilated rather than constricted), and oxygenated blood will be flowing, to make the sensations less painful (refer back to Chapter 4 for a reminder). You can even visualise the blood flowing!

Your support system plays a pivotal role in bolstering your confidence. Discuss your fears openly with your partner, midwife, or doula. They're there to support you emotionally and physically, offering reassurance when anxiety creeps in. Their presence provides a sense of security, knowing you're not alone in this experience. Encourage them to remind you of your strengths and past triumphs when you need a boost. A simple touch or nod from a trusted person can speak volumes, reinforcing your resolve.

You can engage in visualization exercises or what my daughter would call 'manifesting' to prepare for labor day. Imagine the process unfolding smoothly, from the onset of surges/waves/contractions to holding your baby in your arms. Visualize the environment: dim lights, calming music, familiar faces. These mental rehearsals can reduce anxiety by creating a sense of familiarity with what's ahead. You're crafting a mental blueprint that guides you through each stage with assurance.

Of course labor can feel unpredictable, but remember that flexibility is key. Plans might shift, and that's okay. It's like you plan for your beautiful sunny wedding day but then it rains-you pivot and go for plan B. Stay open to adapting as needed, knowing that each decision is made with your well-being and your baby's health in mind. Trust in your healthcare team's expertise while advocating for your preferences.

Remember that pain management strategies are within your grasp. Remind yourself of your birth plan. Reflect on the pain relief options you've explored in this book and practice those techniques regularly. Medications for pain relief are explained in this chapter. You have your own comfort level. Fear and tension from being in too much pain will not help your situation so make sure to advocate for yourself with the help of your supports, and get what you need.

View labor as an opportunity to connect with your inner strength—a strength that's been quietly growing alongside your baby but even before that time. Women are miraculous and have been designed to do this beautiful thing. You are embracing your womanhood to the full! You can acknowledge the presence of worries and anxieties about birth, while choosing not to be ruled by it. You can feel it, let it go and move forward.

UNDERSTANDING LABOR: PHASES AND WHAT TO EXPECT

I already talked about this at the end of Chapter 5 but I am re-iterating here. Understanding the stages of labor can help demystify the process. This is super important to grasp and understand. If you know what is happening to your body, that in itself is calming. My own personal saying in my Doula practice is: Know Your Body, Trust Your Body, Own Your Birth.

Before we go through each stage I want to mention one more thing for delivery day. Eating and drinking! In the pre-labor phase we talked about a phase where contractions can come and go and do not follow a clear pattern where the body is getting ready for labor. I mentioned how important it is to rest in this phase as you will need all your energy imminently. It is also really important to eat when you can and certainly when you feel hungry. Small nutritious meals or smoothies in this phase is so important, and in early labor itself. As time moves on and the cervix dilates you will feel less like eating, and you may even vomit or have some diarrhea (which is entirely normal in labor-it happened to me with my first and was a bit of a mess but it was my body's reaction to moving through into active established labor), but try to keep drinking water between as many contractions as you can.

If you're feeling depleted in the hospital, smoothies are a great option. The 2nd (pushing) stage is shorter if you have adequate nutrition on board.

Some hospitals are against women eating during labor but this can mean that energy levels risk being at an all time low when you need your energy the most, in the 2nd, pushing, stage. The theory behind not eating is that very occasionally, and I'm talking less than 5% of all caesareans, in a true obstetric emergency, have to go under general anaesthetic to have their surgical (caesarean) birth, and if there is food in their stomach, they risk aspirating, causing a life threatening lung infection. The vast majority of women will be giving birth vaginally, or by cesarean with an epidural already on board, meaning no general anaesthetic is needed.

Remember, labor is broken down into 3 stages. 1st is where the cervix softens, thins out and dilates to 10 cm, 2nd is when your baby descends through the open cervix and is born, and 3rd stage is delivery of the placenta. Here is more detail on these stages, which are so important to understand. The more you know about what is happening in your body the more you can literally visualise your baby making its journey to the outside world.

1ST STAGE

This stage which can cause the most confusion can, for simplicity, be divided into 4 stages: early labor, early active labor, well-established active labor and transition

Your surges/waves/contractions start (early labor). They are now regular, getting longer, coming gradually more often and getting more intense. **This is the definition of labor**. If they are uncomfortable but irregular and not getting consistently stronger then this is not labor yet.

These surges/contractions cause:

- The cervix to soften and thin out (called effacement) and to move from a posterior position (meaning pointing towards the back) to an anterior position (facing forward in the vagina)
- Only then, once these changes have happened in early labor, can the cervix dilate (open) up to 10 cm

CERVICAL EFFACEMENT AND DILATION DURING LABOR

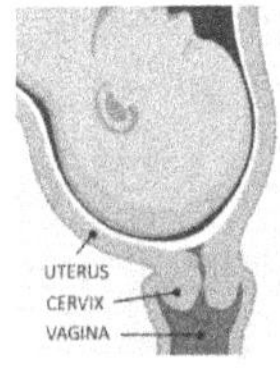

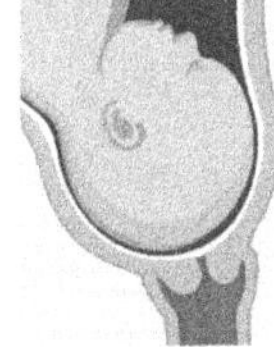

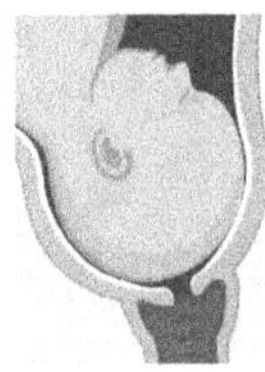

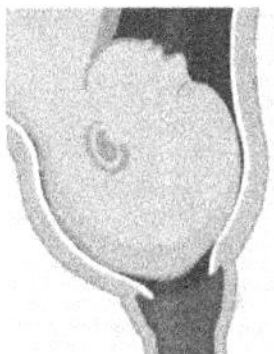

My doula trainer taught it to me this way: think of 100 rubber bands together-they are not going to open. Then think of one rubber band: that can expand easily. The point is the cervix cannot dilate if it's thick.

As this happens, the baby is descending through the birth canal, the bones of the pelvis move apart, including the coccyx moving back, all aided by the hormone relaxin. The baby then rotates and descends. Remember the head 'moulds' at this time, as the parts of the skull are not fused at this point, so the bones mould over each other, to ease the head through the birth canal.

Regular surges/contractions grow stronger, longer, and more frequent, signaling real progress in labor. This is when you really feel the rhythm of labor—the tightening and releasing like waves. Each contraction has a peak, a moment where it feels most intense, then it gradually subsides. During this stage, you might feel pressure in your back or pelvis, depending on your baby's position. Some describe it as a deep ache or strong wave moving through you. Keep as active as you can and change positions, maybe to all fours, if you are experiencing lots of back pain. This could mean that your baby has its spine against your spine (called OP or occipito-posterior) position. All fours is a great option to relieve the back pain that can persist between surges when baby is in this position, and can give the baby some space to move.

Up to 6 cm dilation is known as **early labor** (as long as contractions are regular, getting gradually stronger and gradually becoming more frequent-if not, this is not labor yet). Note: Around 3cm, there is often a small surge of adrenaline as the contractions/surges get stronger- it helps you gather focus and energy for the real work ahead. Some midwives call this the 'take-off phase'.

Get through this with your box breathing, and the oxytocin will take the lead again and labor will deepen. It is an important moment for you to be as focussed as you can on your breathing and visualizations. I honestly believe if you can get through that stage in early active labor and welcome the surges as a way of meeting your baby, from 3cm on when surges are really ramping up, it is a key moment. Remember your box breath during surges/contractions. And the relaxing 4/8 breath in between.

6-8 cm is **active labor**

8-10 cm is what is called '**transition**'. This is the time when adrenaline does come into play. It is probably the most intense moment of labor and it can sometimes overwhelm. I remember saying "I can't do this" to my Mum with my third child at that very point. I knew I was close, but it suddenly seemed overwhelming. She said something along the lines of "don't be silly, 'course you can" and within minutes I was feeling the urge to push. Ride transition and it's like a moment of truth for everyone in the room. Your surges/contractions have reached their peak intensity and frequency, leaving little time between them. It's normal to feel overwhelmed, but galvanize yourself, it's also the shortest phase and is over before you know it! Your body is working tirelessly for that complete dilatation of the cervix, preparing for your baby's descent. The sensations can be powerful, like an unstoppable force moving through you.

WHEN TO GO TO HOSPITAL/BIRTH CENTER

The million dollar question! Of course each couple needs to make sure they have a plan for when you go into labor. Make sure you have an airtight plan for any other children you have, as a mother's instinct will mean things cannot progress until any other children are safe and looked after is number one! Make sure you have your tool kit to hand and start using the tools in it. Change it up if at the next mile marker your current tool isn't working so well. Change positions, change the music etc etc. The rule of thumb for doulas is to call them or meet at the hospital, whatever the plan happens to be, at 5-1-1 or even 4-1-1 if you are coping well. You may well be at 3+ cm dilated at this point). This means contractions/surges/waves are 4-5 minutes apart, for at least 1 hour and they are 1 minute long. Some hospitals will even say 3-1-1. Honestly, if you can stay at home until 4-1-1 or 3-1-1 particularly in the US, you are more likely to have less intervention. It is a good idea to ask your provider when you should go into hospital once your waters break. Some will say you can stay at home for a few hours. There is not necessarily a huge hurry as long as the fluid has no smell and is clear and baby's movement are good. However, be aware the waters breaking can increase contraction intensity quite a bit so I would certainly be ready if this happens as things may be moving on at a quicker pace.

I would like to emphasize this-if your choice is to limit intervention as much as possible, and you plan an unmedicated birth, then stay at home until you reach these time markers. Labor will often slow down when you go to an unfamiliar place, and you will be more comfortable with your own things around you at home. You will be free to eat and drink as you need and will maybe also feel more comfortable with natural measures to help labor like nipple stimulation (enhances oxytocin), sex (semen contains prostaglandins that can help with cervical ripening, orgasm releases oxytocin). Of course walking and upright movement are also great for moving the baby deeper into the pelvis and supports your body's process. There are many myths about what other things might stimulate labor. The only ones that have evidence behind them are dates (you can eat 6 per day from about 37 weeks), raspberry leaf tea for strengthening the muscle tone in the uterus and therefore making contractions more efficient once they begin, and possibly evening primrose oil to help soften the cervix.

A note about your journey into the hospital. It is essential that you continue your breathing techniques during the drive to hospital. Remain focussed and in your zone while your partner/friend/relative drives. Make sure they are completely aware of the route. Remember to bring a towel in the car in case your waters break on the way. There may be traffic. I love hearing my sister's story of staying in her deeply relaxed state in the back of the car on all fours, while her husband drove 40 minutes through the London rush hour. Her labor continued to progress with no delay.

2ND STAGE

Finally, the moment you've been waiting for—the delivery of your baby. You will suddenly start feeling this overwhelming urge to push. With each push, you channel every ounce of energy into bringing your child into the world. It's an awe-inspiring moment when effort and instinct converge.

Remember that here you must go with the urge to push and use your welcome breath. Never ever hold your breath! Note: I recently heard that in the US women are sometimes asked not to push or to stop pushing for the doctor to arrive in time-in my view this is next to impossible and is not something I would ever condone. At this point trust your body that it absolutely knows what to do and you need to enter this phase without fear, and let your body lead. It is an extraordinary moment. The nurse or midwife should know how to help you control your pushes as the head is born, to minimize any tearing.

Take a full breath in and then a really long exhale through your mouth, with your lips pursed. Keep your jaw and neck relaxed so that all the energy is concentrated lower in your body. You might want to make a low sound, a moo or a hum or whatever comes out, but a long sound to go with the breath. I certainly did, and it was animalistic for sure. It may feel like you need to make a bowel movement. This is exactly where you concentrate your breath. I literally loved this phase. For me it didn't take too long, the sensation to push is a strong one which you want to make sure you do not resist. In this phase more than anything, I think I realised how incredible the human body is, all the elements of pregnancy and labor come together for this concentrated movement of your baby on its final journey through the birth canal. I just went with the sensation and knew that soon I would meet my baby, it was exhilarating. Listen to your midwife or doctor here. They can help prevent tearing, by helping you control your breathing as the head 'crowns'. Remember, if you do have an epidural you may not feel this incredible sensation-it really does help to shorten this stage if you can feel this urge, so you can even ask the nurses to turn down the epidural so you feel that sensation to help the second stage.

3RD STAGE

Once your baby is born, you enter the third stage: delivering the placenta. This can seem unexpected as you meet and cuddle and maybe even feed your baby for the first time but it's an essential element of this process. You will feel further surges to help expel the placenta, completing the birth process. It is at this stage that the final attachment between mother and baby is cut, the umbilical cord, which has transferred blood and nutrients from mother to baby all through the pregnancy.

MONITORING IN LABOR

It is important to mention this even on your birth plan. Often women, once they get to hospital, are monitored with a strap around their belly, which relays contractions and baby's heartbeat.

This is called **continuous electronic fetal monitoring** (CEFM) — this means constant monitoring of the baby's heart rate and your contractions with a strap placed around your belly. While it feels reassuring to keep tabs on the baby, the latest research shows that CEFM in *low-risk labours* can actually restrict mobility, raise intervention rates (like forceps, vacuum or cesarean), and **doesn't improve** long-term outcomes for most babies. Always ask your care team when, how, and *why monitoring* is used, so you stay informed and mobile. Often hospitals can engage in INTERMITTENT monitoring of your baby which maybe be a good compromise so that you don't feel so restricted.

- If you are classified *low-risk* (healthy pregnancy, baby in head-down position, labour progressing normally), you could ask whether intermittent auscultation (listening periodically rather than constant monitoring) is an option.
- If monitoring is recommended, ask if you can use **wireless or portable** monitors so you stay free to change positions, move around or use birthing balls — these formats showed better comfort and mobility.
- Remember that the purpose of monitoring is to help detect genuine concerns when they arise — and that more monitoring can mean more action, and more action can mean more interventions.

PAIN MANAGEMENT OPTIONS: MAKING INFORMED CHOICES

Pain during labor can be a profound, often intense experience, and managing it is deeply personal and unique. The array of choices available reflects the diverse experiences and preferences of individuals embarking on this extraordinary journey. The key lies in discovering what aligns with your personal comfort and strength, empowering you to feel in control throughout the process. Remember all the options we talked about in the NHS birth plan template. We will look at all these now. Make sure to ask your hospital, birth center or midwife about which of these might be possible in your country and specific birth facility.

NATURAL METHODS

Remember when we were talking about Calm Birthing techniques in Chapter 4. The calmer you are, the more you will be tapping into the parasympathetic nervous system, the more the blood vessels supplying the muscle of the uterus will be dilated, and blood will flow, causing a reduction in pain. The **deep relaxation/'hypnobirthing'** method has gained attention for its ability to tap into the mind's potential to induce a state of calm and focused concentration. This method emphasizes deep relaxation techniques designed to help you manage labor pain more naturally and intuitively. By redirecting your focus, hypnobirthing aims to replace fear and tension with deep relaxation and calm, allowing the body to respond to labor in a constructive and harmonious way. Make sure to re-read Chapter 4 and practice the techniques mentioned. Hypnobirthing has proven to reduce interventions, pain relief and caesarean sections.

Breathing techniques in general, like those used in the calm birthing techniques discussed in Chapter 4, are a cornerstone of natural pain management in labor. The consistent pace of breathing serves as an anchor, synchronizing with the body's natural labor rhythm. Each controlled inhale and exhale guides relaxation, dispelling tension rather like waves receding from the shore.

Hydrotherapy, with its soothing and enveloping nature, is another method embraced by many during labor. The comforting embrace of warm water creates a buoyancy that serves to reduce the intensity of contractions/surges, making the pressures of labor more manageable. A water birth can transform the atmosphere into one that echoes serenity and peace. The buoyancy not only supports the body but allows for graceful, fluid movement, helping to ease transitions between contractions.

TENS (transcutaneous electrical nerve stimulation) **machine** is a small, handheld device that sends gentle pulses through pads on your lower back to help block pain signals and boost your body's own endorphins. It works best if you start in early labor, turning the intensity up during each surge and down between them; you stay fully mobile and can combine it with breathing, massage, or movement. Many people report it takes the "edge" off without drugs and I would agree with that, I used one with my first delivery. Don't use it in water (disconnect from the pads on your back and remove the pads before a shower or bath and you can then stick them back on after) and avoid use it if you have a pacemaker or implanted defibrillator; use caution with epilepsy and place pads only on the back (not the abdomen or neck). Overall research shows modest pain relief and high satisfaction for those who like non-pharmacologic options.

DRUGS

In early labor you can use tylenol/paracetamol for mid relief.

The most effective drug option in terms of relief from the pain of labor almost entirely, is epidural analgesia which provides excellent pain relief without increasing cesarean rates, though it can lengthen the second stage and raise the chance of an assisted vaginal birth. What is important though, is that this is your experience, and only you can experience what your body is feeling and your response to that. My friend said she felt so much pressure not to get an epidural. This can cause more issues. Let go of expectations, try not to feel any pressure, as that can cause more tension and therefore increase pain. Be in the experience itself and the choice will become clear to you.

This table give clear pros and cons which are worth considering:

BENEFITS	NOTES
Most effective pain relief available	Provides significant reduction in labor pain without affecting consciousness.
Can help with exhaustion or long labors	Allows the mother to rest, conserve energy, and stay calm, which may support progress in prolonged labor.
Improves ability to tolerate medical interventions	Particularly helpful if oxytocin (pitocin) augmentation or assisted delivery becomes necessary.
Does not increase caesarean section rates	Modern low-dose epidurals have not been shown to increase the chance of C-section
Can be helpful for high-risk pregnancies	Beneficial in cases of high blood pressure, preeclampsia, or anticipated complicated delivery, as it stabilizes stress responses.

Provides anesthesia if cesarean becomes necessary	An epidural already in place can often be used for a surgical birth, avoiding general anesthesia.

CONS/RISKS	NOTES
Can lengthen second stage (pushing)	Reduced urge to push and decreased pelvic sensation can prolong the pushing phase.
Increased likelihood of assisted (instrumental) vaginal birth	Higher use of forceps or vacuum is associated with epidural analgesia.

Reduced bladder sensation requiring urinary catheterisation	Because the epidural affects pelvic nerves, many women are unable to feel a full bladder and may need an intermittent or indwelling catheter. A full bladder can obstruct the baby's descent if not emptied regularly. These are also used as mothers have decreased mobility so cannot safely go to the bathroom when the epidural starts working
Possible drop in blood pressure	Epidurals can cause maternal hypotension, which is managed with fluids or medication.
Limited mobility	Epidurals usually require continuous fetal monitoring and staying in bed.
Affects pushing sensation	The reduced ability to feel contractions may require coached pushing.

Small risk of side effects	Headache from dural puncture, itching, shivering, or fever may occur in some women.
Potential impact on birth hormones	Reduced natural oxytocin release may affect the physiological rhythm of labor.

An **epidural** works by delivering a local anaesthetic/ numbing drug (for instance bupivacaine) continuously through a plastic 'catheter', into the 'epidural space', accessed through your back, which is the area just outside/ near where the spinal cord lies. The drug blocks the nerves that carry pain signals from the lower body to the brain, so causing numbness and a lack of pain, although you can still usually feel pressure. The timing of an epidural is important as if it is placed too early in labor, they can slow the process down. As detailed in the table above, it is worth noting again that it is important that women have fluids before an epidural is inserted. Epidurals can cause a drop in blood pressure so the fluids help to keep the blood pressure stable and prevent this. Otherwise emergency interventions can kick in that were not necessary.

A few hospitals in the UK and USA offer a 'walking' or mobile epidural — a different version of the standard epidural that aims to reduce pain but allow more movement and position changes during labour. In these, a local anaesthetic is still used but at a lower dose. Then added to that is a low dose of an opioid such as fentanyl which means you may preserve more leg strength and ability to change position which is so critical in labor. However, walking is not always allowed in practice, monitoring is still required, and pain relief may be less extensive than a full epidural.

Systemic opioids are also sometimes used (for instance fentanyl, morphine, nalbuphine or in the UK pethidine/ diamorphine/remifentanil, given intravenously or into the muscle) offer modest analgesia but can cause maternal nausea/sedation and transient newborn respiratory depression or drowsiness, and although at the right time in labor these drugs can work well and give you some rest, they must be used with caution.

Nitrous oxide or 'laughing gas' is used widely in the UK and in some hospitals in the USA. It is a gas, (usually 50% nitrous oxide and 50% oxygen) which you breathe in through a mask and provides mild-to-moderate pain relief. It has the great advantage of preserving your mobility, It works on the central nervous system by altering your pain perception, inducing calm, relaxation and sometimes mild euphoria, hence the common name of 'laughing gas'. It wears off within minutes of you breathing it in but can be effectively be used during contractions/surges as it works quickly usually within 30 seconds of breathing it in.

PARTNER'S ROLE IN THE DELIVERY ROOM: ESSENTIAL SUPPORT TACTICS

Partners (and doulas if you are using one) are so important in labor, providing both reassurance and practical help during this intense time. Their presence eases anxiety and keeps your preferences central, acting as advocates with medical staff and ensuring you feel heard throughout the process. Doulas can also help manage your birth partner's needs, and make sure they are working effectively.

Emotional support often makes the biggest impact—holding a hand, offering affirmations, relaxation and massage techniques or simply listening fosters connection and calm. Partners and doulas also provide practical aid by timing contractions, offering massages or counterpressure, helping with movement and positions, or using comfort tools like warm compresses and birth balls to ease tension and aid progress.

Preparation before labor strengthens this role: talking through expectations, practicing comfort measures, and learning about interventions equips partners to stay composed when plans change. In moments of unpredictability, adaptability and calm reassurance become invaluable, grounding you as circumstances shift.

Ultimately, labor is a shared journey. With presence, attentiveness, and flexibility, partners turn a daunting process into a supportive and empowering experience—

one that deepens bonds and celebrates teamwork at the start of parenthood.

My partner is not one for hospitals and all thing medical but he came into his own from my very first experience of birth. It seemed instinctual. During the second stage, he held me up from behind, on the floor, so that I could use the counterpressure to push my baby out. He was my partner and doula rolled into one. Forever grateful that he had those instincts and acted on them in this animal moment. No words, just this magnificent support.

INTERVENTIONS IN THE BIRTHING PROCESS

We have talked about the stages of labor and pain relief options. You may deliver your baby naturally, using natural pain relief measures, or use drugs or an epidural.

As we know, babies don't always follow the path you may have planned for them, at the end of pregnancy, and beyond! It is important for me to mention and inform you about various interventions which may need to take place in order that your baby is delivered safely.

Remember, some of these interventions may well be planned before labor for good reason, but some of them can take place while you are in labor. Sometimes decisions need to be made quickly, which can be distressing. I believe, the more information you have going into this, the better. Understanding potential variations in labor can ease anxiety. Sometimes interventions like inductions or assisted deliveries become necessary to ensure everyone's safety. It's just part of the unpredictability of birth. Trust that your body knows what to do, even if plans shift unexpectedly.

Labor's unpredictability means embracing flexibility. Duration varies widely; some experience quick labors while others take their time. Interventions may be necessary for safety or comfort—remember they're tools to support you, not measures of success or failure.

Ultimately, understanding labor's phases equips you with knowledge and confidence as you prepare for this remarkable experience in bringing new life into the world. And the more you and your partner are prepared for possible interventions the better. A doula can also help advocate for you and help you understand implications and help you make sound decisions when your birth plan has to change.

INDUCTION OF LABOR

There are many reasons why an induction of labor may be called for, and it is important to understand that this could change your birth experience. Some pregnant women are offered induction before their due date. In some it is medically necessary, in some it is not, and some women are induced-or induction drugs are used-once a woman is already in labor, to hasten the process, where they may have been given the diagnosis of 'failure to progress'. This in itself is a phrase I would hope would not be uttered anywhere near a pregnant or laboring woman. There is no failure in this process, and it is important for birth partners-partners and doulas, try to shield women from this kind of negative talk during labor. Anything can set off a delay in a laboring woman who is trying to stay 'in the zone' of her surges and progress, even the turning on of a light or too much noise.

WHAT IS INDUCTION AND WHY IS IT OFFERED?

Induction of labor (IOL) means using medications and/or procedures to start labor before it begins on its own. It's offered when continuing pregnancy is likely riskier than giving birth—common reasons include pregnancy going past term, high blood pressure/preeclampsia, diabetes, waters breaking without labor (called pre-labor rupture of membranes or PROM), concerns about fetal growth, reduced amniotic fluid or medical conditions in the mother. There is always a balance between not wanting to deliver too early when the body is not ready, and protecting both mother and child. Research shows that even though 37 weeks is considered 'term', more babies born before 39 weeks are admitted in the newborn period with breathing and sometimes feeding problems so unless medically indicated for the mother, reaching 39 weeks is preferable.

There is a drive in the USA particularly to induce mothers at 39 weeks electively, meaning a planned induction. This has particularly been the case since the ARRIVE paper was published, in the USA, in 2018. With the particular sample of mothers it used, it showed no increase in cesarean sections, and even a decrease, and no worse outcomes for babies where labor was induced at 39 weeks, which led to US guidance that this kind of elective induction at 39 weeks was a reasonable option if families wanted to consider it. Papers have been published analysing the sample of patients used and the conclusions that were reached. It is important to consider a couple of things. There is concern over selection bias in the study, that the sample of women in the study were not representative of the overall study population. And so it is not clear whether the treatment and outcomes would have been the same in those eligible for the study but who decided not to participate. (22,533 women were eligible to participate and only 6106 took part). It is suggested that further rigorous study take place before any general policy change takes place.

In the UK, induction is offered and generally advised at 41 weeks.

If a woman's water has broken and labor has not started, this is called premature rupture of membranes (PROM).

For this, induction is advised within 24 hours to reduce any infection risk.

HOW INDUCTION IS DONE (METHODS YOU MAY BE OFFERED)

If when you come in for induction the cervix is not ready to dilate (you can look back at the picture on page 163 remember the cervix has to soften and efface before dilating) then you can have drugs inserted into the vagina which will initiate this '**cervical ripening**' or a mechanical method is used.

- **Prostaglandins** (often a drug called dinoprostone or low-dose misoprostol in some settings) soften the cervix.

or:

- **Mechanical methods** can be used: (a balloon or Foley catheter) gently open the cervix and can safely be done as an outpatient in certain low-risk patients.

or:

- **Amniotomy** (breaking the waters)

or:

- **Membrane sweeping** at term can reduce the need for formal induction and may bring on labor sooner. Though it can be uncomfortable and doesn't always work, it is a safe method to try, with no increase in cesarean and less than 1 in a 1000 risk of serious infection. It involves the HCP inserting one or two fingers into the cervix, and using a continuous circular sweeping motion to free the membrane from the cervix.

or:

- **Oxytocin** (also known as Pitocin) is then used, and given through a vein, to stimulate contractions, after the cervix is ripe.

WHAT TO EXPECT AND BENEFITS V RISKS

Induction can take time—often a day or more—especially for first births with an unripe cervix. It is very important to allow **adequate time** for early (latent) labor where the cervix is preparing/softening and then sufficient oxytocin before declaring a failed induction which would lead to a Cesarean. This approach reduces unnecessary cesareans.

- **Potential benefits:** it is possible there is a lower chance of cesarean and fewer hypertensive complications-both conclusions from the contested ARRIVE study, and—when done at or beyond term—there are shown to be small reductions in perinatal death and admission to the Neonatal Intensive Care Unit (NICU).

- **Potential downsides:** longer hospital stay for some, more need for continuous monitoring/ drugs into your vein, stronger contractions with oxytocin (affecting pain relief choices), and rare complications tied to specific methods.

SPECIAL SITUATIONS

- **Previous cesarean (planning a vaginal birth after cesarean, commonly known as a VBAC):** Mechanical methods and cautious oxytocin may be used; misoprostol is avoided as there is a higher chance of rupture of the uterus with this drug. Each pregnant mother will be assessed individually to make sure this is the right course of action. 60-80% of VBAC's are successful, particularly if you have had a previously vaginal birth and some research shows that spontaneous labor has more successful outcomes in VBAC than inducing the mother.

- **Older maternal age ($\geq$35 years):** UK data show 39-week induction **doesn't raise cesarean risk**; counseling often includes discussion of stillbirth risk trends with advancing gestation. Again each case is unique and discussion with your HCP is essential. I had my last baby at 43 years and there was no discussion about induction, and that was in Los Angeles.

As I have mentioned in this book before, knowledge is power! This is your body and your baby. Go to your HCP with information that you have gained from this book and any other reputable sources. If you feel like it, you can take a deeper dive into the papers cited in my reference section. I would heavily caution using social media as a source of information for this kind of decision making.

SHARED DECISION-MAKING: QUESTIONS TO ASK IF YOUR DOCTOR SUGGESTS INDUCTION

- Can I just be clear on the reasons you want me to be induced? Are there alternatives?
- How "ripe" is my cervix and what ripening option fits my circumstances? (The cervix being 'ready' is key for dilatation of your cervix. But you know that already!)
- What's our plan and **time allowances** before calling the induction "failed"?
- Can any steps (e.g. balloon catheter) be done as an **outpatient**?
- How do my conditions (e.g. high blood pressure, prior cesarean, breech) change timing or method?

Always use the acronym BRAINS for all your pregnancy and birth decision making:

B   what are the **BENEFITS** of this intervention

R   what are the **RISKS** of this intervention

A   what are the **ALTERNATIVES** to this intervention

I   what is your **INSTINCT**

N   what if I do **NOTHING**

S   I think I want a **SECOND OPINION** ** this **S** can also remind you to **SMILE** and laugh, which will help the flow of oxytocin, relax your jaw and help move baby down.

(Even if you just remember the first three, your BRA, that will be great!)

BOTTOM LINE

For many healthy first-time pregnancies at term, **planned induction can be as safe as waiting**, with a possible **modest reduction in cesarean birth** and fewer hypertensive disorders (see ARRIVE study), but remember the limitations of this study. The **best timing** and **method** depend on your health, pregnancy details, and preferences. Make sure you have your voice heard and consider all the options. Just be aware if you have to have an induction the early stages can be quite prolonged as the doctors are having to get your cervix primed artificially (with drugs or mechanical methods) before the cervix can dilate. Talk to your doctor about starting your induction as an outpatient.

ASSISTED OR INSTRUMENTAL VAGINAL BIRTH (FORCEPS OR VACUUM/"VENTOUSE")

- **What it is & when it's used**

  An assisted vaginal birth uses forceps or a vacuum cup to help deliver the baby—typically to hurry up the birth for worry about the baby or the mother (for instance exhaustion, prolonged second stage, medical conditions where a shorter pushing phase is safer). Your HCP-a doctor/ obstetrician in this case, in the US and UK should confirm the position of the baby and assess the safety of the procedure. An epidural is used for anesthesia in this case, so that there is no delay if the delivery needs to proceed to a Cesarean.

- **Vacuum vs forceps: how they differ**

  There are two main types of assistance: vacuum (also called ventouse) and forceps. Both are designed to gently support your baby's journey through the birth canal while keeping you and your baby safe.

- Forceps look a bit like smooth, curved spoons that cradle your baby's head. They often make birth quicker once they are in place — helpful if your baby needs to be born promptly.
- Vacuum (ventouse) uses a small soft cup and gentle suction to guide the baby out with your contractions. It usually causes less stretching or tearing for the mother, though babies can have a small temporary bruise or swelling on the scalp that fades within a few days.

Both methods are well-studied and widely used. The right choice depends on the situation, your baby's position, and your care provider's experience. Serious complications are *very rare* with either technique.

These kinds of deliveries often involve what is called an **episiotomy**.

An episiotomy is a small surgical cut made in the perineum (the tissue between the vaginal opening and the anus) during the pushing stage of birth, to widen the opening. It's not routine anymore but reserved for specific situations—most often with assisted/instrumental births (vacuum or forceps), when there's concern about the baby needing to be born quickly, or if the perineum isn't stretching despite good efforts.

It's done under local anesthesia, then stitched with dissolvable sutures after birth. If an epidural is in place the local anaesthetic won't be needed but they may want to top up the epidural before proceeding, and if it is not working consistently they may use local anesthetic as well. Possible downsides include **pain, bleeding, infection, and the cut extending into a deeper tear** (risk is higher with a straight **midline** cut than a **mediolateral-from the middle going out to the side-** one). Most people heal well within a few weeks with perineal care, ice, and pain relief as advised by their provider.

The most important thing is that your team will always talk you through what's happening, explain why an assisted birth might be recommended, and make sure you and your baby are cared for safely throughout the process. Remember **BRAINS** when you are considering this procedure.

THE BENEFITS OF THE JOURNEY THROUGH THE BIRTH CANAL

Before we move on I wanted to spend a minute on some interesting facts about the advantages of a baby's passage through the birth canal, if that is a possibility in your particular situation

The passage through the birth canal does offer remarkable benefits for both mother and baby. As a baby moves through the vagina, the gentle compression of the chest helps to get rid of fluid from their lungs, preparing them for breathing air immediately after birth. At the same time, this physical process stimulates vital hormonal and circulatory transitions that support smoother adaptation to life outside the womb.

Perhaps even more fascinating is the transfer of beneficial bacteria from mother to baby during vaginal birth. As the baby passes through the birth canal, they are coated in the mother's vaginal and gut (completely harmless) bacteria, which helps to seed the baby's developing immune system and gut health. Almost like a "starter culture" for the baby's own immune and digestive systems. Research shows that babies born vaginally tend to have more diverse natural/ healthy bacteria early in life — something associated with stronger immunity and lower risks of allergies, asthma, and autoimmune conditions later on.

Note that 'vaginal seeding' can be done in cesarean section, where you swab a newborn with the mother's vaginal fluids, in hopes of transferring beneficial bacteria that babies usually receive during vaginal birth.

As labour progresses naturally, the mother's body releases **oxytocin** — the hormone of love, trust, and connection — in rhythmic waves. We've talked about this quite a bit. This same hormone helps the uterus contract effectively and stimulates endorphins, the body's natural pain relievers, fostering a sense of focus, calm, and even euphoria at the moment of birth. When the baby emerges and is placed skin-to-skin, those oxytocin levels surge even higher, helping to cement emotional bonding and stimulate early breastfeeding.

For the baby, the gradual hormonal shifts during labour — including exposure to maternal oxytocin, adrenaline, and cortisol — help prepare the brain and body for alertness after birth. Babies born vaginally often show greater responsiveness and calm engagement in the first hours of life, ready to seek eye contact and latch for feeding.

This hormonal cascade or cocktail if you like, is a biologically orchestrated process that not only ensures physical transition but also lays the emotional foundation for attachment and maternal confidence.

CESAREAN OR SURGICAL BIRTH

Next we will talk about Cesarean or surgical birth. There are circumstances where this cannot be avoided, and as I have mentioned throughout this book, at the end of the day, we want a healthy baby, a safe delivery for you, the mother, and a positive experience. This can happen however your baby is delivered. Many women talk of having to have an 'emergency cesarean'. Make sure if this is you, that the doctors explain exactly what the emergency is. Often when asked, women don't exactly know why it was done. Make sure you always use the BRAINS acronym, to work through with your HCP the best choice for you and your family and also so that you understand clearly why a surgical birth is decided upon.

A note about cesareans before we continue. I have to note the wide disparity in cesarean rates among different countries, and in this case specifically the USA and the UK. In 2023, the last year I could get accurate data before publishing this book, the cesarean rate in the USA was 32.3%. It was lower for first time mothers, at 22.8% although there was a gradual rise from 2019-2021 in younger women. The American College of Obstetrics and Gynecology are trying to safely reduce the number of cesarean births, with improved prenatal care including being aware of known risk factors and detecting any issues with the baby including positioning, in good time, to make sure issues are actively addressed before labor begins. Also heartening was a quote from this particular paper that health care teams needed to have a 'solid understanding of physiologic birth processes'! Yes, exactly.

Historically in the UK, the cesarean rate has consistently been lower than the USA, around one in 4 births (25%). However, in my recent research I have found a worrying trend that in the latest statistics from 2023, the rate of cesarean section in the UK even surpassed that in the USA, at 38.9%. This is being addressed at a national level. There are ongoing issues in the UK, with news and various investigative surveys reporting incredible work by individuals in maternity units but that units are often understaffed and underfunded.

There are certainly issues in both countries and inequities can be stark. Changes clearly need to be made and it seems that in the USA and the UK maternity services are being looked at, and I hope we will see improvements. The fact remains, and I truly believe this, women of any background, race or ideology, who are listened to, who can express their hopes, fears, anxieties and realities, are more likely to go into pregnancy and birth with a calmer and more positive attitude. I do believe this positively affects outcomes.

All statistics quoted in these pages are cited in the reference section.

Now back to the details!

Cesareans are **planned** in certain circumstances:

- If the placenta is blocking the cervix (placenta previa-this is uncommon, at only 0.5% of pregnancies), or is low lying
- Certain maternal conditions, like some heart conditions, severe preeclampsia, prior uterine surgery)
- Multiple pregnancy
- Breech where the baby's bottom or feet are nearest the birth canal rather than the head-this occurs in 3-4% of pregnancies and often your

HCP will try to turn the baby (called external cephalic version-ECV) but it doesn't always work

Vaginal Breech Birth: A recent analysis of studies relating to vaginal breech delivery shows that a vaginal breech birth can possibly cause a small rise in perinatal mortality (death of the baby that occur around the time of birth) and birth trauma but that in terms of maternal morbidity (complications/conditions in the mother that are caused or worsened by pregnancy or childbirth), a vaginal breech birth was safer than a cesarean delivery. This, of course, poses an ethical dilemma and one that will be highly individual in each case of breech presentation and needs to be discussed in detail with your team. With an experienced and well-trained provider and a healthy mother with no other complications, vaginal breech delivery can be a very viable option for a mother who would prefer not to have a surgical birth. One of the most worrying aspects to me, particulalry in the US, is the increasing lack of experience Healthcare Professionals are receiving in vaginal breech birth. Many have not attended one in years, particularly as a result of the flawed Term Breech Trial that came out in the year 2000, which suggested cesarean was safer but the trial had many issues and in fact six years later the ACOG determined that vaginal breech delivery was acceptable in certain cases. In fact they still maintain this, that if a ECV (turning procedure) does not work, then if the mother wants a vaginal breech delivery, then this should be offered and carried out by a skilled, experienced HCP in a hospital setting. The loss of skill is clearly an issue. A friend of mine in Los Angeles, who wanted a vaginal breech birth eight years ago, found only 4 doctors in the entire LA metropolis, who would deliver her baby. She had a successful unmedicated vaginal breech birth using hypnobirthing techniques.

Or:

Cesarean can be **unplanned or an emergency** during labour for concerns about the mother or baby.

WHAT TO EXPECT

A planned cesarean is normally carried out under a spinal or epidural anaesthetic, so you're awake but pain-free. Your birth partner can usually be beside you, and most hospitals encourage skin-to-skin contact and early breastfeeding immediately after birth, right in the operating room.

Many women describe a planned cesarean as surprisingly calm and positive. You'll be surrounded by a supportive team, music is often allowed, and your baby is brought to you right away. In different hospitals there will be different protocols on cesareans. Always ask what the protocols are so you know what to expect.

The focus is on safety, but should also be on connection, and care — not on losing the "birth experience," but simply doing it differently. Make sure to ask your hospital how close they can come to what is called a '**calm cesarean**' or women-centered cesarean. These would include these kinds of measures:

- Quiet environment
- Softer lighting
- Staff introducing themselves
- Make sure IV is placed in convenient place (usually hand or lower forearm so upper arm/elbow free) and that any ECG/EKG pads off the chest (can be placed on sides of torso, or upper shoulders/clavicle area
- Your music playing
- Partner allowed at head of bed
- Doula allowed in the room of you have one
- Obsterician slowly lifts baby's head out to mimic the squeezing effect of vaginal birth, to expel fluid from the baby's lungs
- Once head delivered, mother's bed is tipped slightly up (so mother lying slightly higher) and drape lowered so mother can see her baby
- Delayed cord clamping, then possibly partner cuts cord
- Then baby lifted over to go straight on mothers chest, skin-to skin. If mother unable then partner can do skin to skin right away
- Baby checks done while lying on mother's chest

HOW A CESAREAN BIRTH IS DONE & PREVENTING INFECTION

A cesarean birth usually involves a small horizontal incision low on the abdomen—just above the bikini line. This is the standard approach because it heals well and leaves a discreet scar.

Before the operation begins, you'll be given antibiotics through a drip to prevent infection. These are carefully chosen and dose-adjusted for your body weight. In the United States, a medicine called *cefazolin* is commonly used; in the United Kingdom, the exact antibiotic may vary slightly depending on hospital policy.

If your cesarean happens after labour has started or after your waters have broken, studies show that adding a small dose of another antibiotic (*azithromycin*) can further lower the risk of infection for mothers.

After your baby is born, most hospitals now encourage skin-to-skin contact right in theatre and support early breastfeeding just like after a vaginal delivery, as long as you and your baby are well. These moments help stimulate oxytocin release, calm your baby, and promote bonding— just as they do after vaginal birth. Remember to review all the measures above to help facilitate a cesarean delivery experience that works for you and your partner.

RISKS AND LONG-TERM CONSIDERATIONS

A cesarean is a very safe operation, but like any surgery, it carries a few short-term risks. These include:

- Bleeding (haemorrhage)
- Infection of the wound or uterus
- Blood clots (VTE)
- Injury to nearby organs (rare)

Babies born by cesarean, particularly before 39 weeks, can sometimes have a little more breathing difficulty at first, because they haven't experienced the natural compression of the lungs that happens during vaginal birth.

It's important to remember that most women recover very well from cesarean birth and go on to have healthy future pregnancies.

VBAC: VAGINAL BIRTH AFTER CESAREAN

If you've had one previous cesarean with a low, horizontal (transverse) incision, you can consider a VBAC for a subsequent baby—a *vaginal birth after cesarean.*

For many women, attempting a vaginal birth after a prior cesarean is a safe and reasonable option. About 60–80% of women who try for a VBAC have a successful vaginal birth.

The main risk—a uterine scar opening or rupture—is *rare* (around 0.5–1%), but it requires that the hospital be ready to perform an immediate cesarean if needed. Because of this, planning and discussion with your care team early in pregnancy are essential.

You can talk with your midwife or doctor about whether VBAC is right for you, and what support is available in your chosen birth setting.

I appreciate there has been much to discuss about the actual birth of your baby and any interventions you may need.

Once your baby is finally born, there are just a few final items to discuss about the 3rd stage of labor-when you deliver the placenta and just after!

Make sure your partner/birth support knows what you wish for and write it in the back of the book or in a separate birth plan. I will discuss these here: delayed cord clamping, medication for the 3rd stage, vitamin K for the baby, eye drops for baby and cord blood storage.

ACTIVE OR PHYSIOLOGICAL MANAGEMENT OF THE THIRD STAGE

Research indicates that using a medication like oxytocin during the third stage of labor can in some circumstances, help the uterus contract more quickly and effectively. In some cases it can significantly reduce the possibility of heavy bleeding after the baby is born (postpartum hemorrhage). This is what's known as active management. While active management offers important safety benefits—particularly in preventing excessive bleeding—it also introduces medical intervention at a physiological stage of birth.

Physiological (natural) management allows the placenta to be delivered without medications, relying on the body's natural hormonal processes, along with controlled cord traction and uterine massage which helps the uterus to contract after the baby is born-this helps the uterus shrink and stops bleeding from the area where the placenta was attached. This option is often chosen by women planning a low-intervention birth.

Both approaches are safe when clinically appropriate, but active management offers greater reduction of risk in preventing hemorrhage. This is something you should discuss with your partner and your HCP.

DELAYED CORD CLAMPING (DCC)

Delayed cord clamping (DCC) for vigorous babies, with good color and a strong cry, even if they are premature, means waiting before clamping the umbilical cord—typically 30–60 seconds in the US and at least 1 minute in the UK, with longer delays when feasible and the baby is well. High-quality evidence shows DCC raises the newborn blood count (hemoglobin) at birth and improves iron stores at 3–6 months; in preterm infants it reduces the need for blood transfusions and other complications. There can be a small increase in jaundice in these newborns requiring phototherapy treatment, so it's important to be aware and treat it as necessary. Midwives and Doctors may shorten the cord clamping delay if urgent resuscitation is needed, but for most births DCC is a simple step with meaningful short- and medium-term benefits and should be encouraged. This has become normal practice in many places now, and I wish it had been more widely practiced back when I was having my babies!

VITAMIN K AFTER BIRTH

Newborns have very low vitamin K stores, and without prophylaxis a small but real risk of vitamin K deficiency bleeding (VKDB)—including late, life-threatening bleeding in the brain—exists. High-quality evidence shows that a single dose through the muscle (typically given in the baby's thigh) can significantly reduce VKDB compared to not having this dose, and is also more effective than a single oral dose. (You can give a few doses by mouth which can also be as effective if you don't miss any). There has been some debate in the past about an association between this vitamin K injection and childhood leukemia but this has now been disproven when looking at large amounts of data.

WHAT ABOUT EYE DROPS FOR MY BABY

Newborn eye drops (ocular prophylaxis). The goal is to prevent ophthalmia neonatorum, especially from Neisseria gonorrhoeae (a sexually transmitted disease) which can cause rapid corneal damage in a newborn. In the United States, universal prophylaxis with 0.5% erythromycin ophthalmic ointment to both eyes soon after birth is recommended and is even mandated in most states in the USA.

In the United Kingdom, routine universal eye prophylaxis is not standard practice; in the UK the emphasis is on prenatal screening and treatment for gonorrhoea/chlamydia and urgent assessment/treatment of any neonatal conjunctivitis rather than blanket drops.

WHAT IS ALL THIS ABOUT CORD BLOOD STORAGE

After your baby is born, a small amount of blood remains in the umbilical cord and placenta. This cord blood contains special stem cells — that can develop into any cell in the human body. These stem cells can be used to treat certain rare blood, immune, and metabolic disorders, such as some forms of leukemia and sickle-cell disease.

Because of this, parents are sometimes offered the option to store or donate their baby's cord blood. There are two main ways this can happen:

- Public donation – The cord blood is collected and stored in a public cord blood bank, where it can help other patients in need of a stem-cell transplant. This is a generous, community-minded choice — much like donating blood — and it's the option most professional organizations recommend.
- Private storage – Some families choose to pay to store their baby's cord blood for their own future use. However, major medical bodies such as the American College of Obstetricians and Gynecologists (ACOG) and the American Academy of Pediatrics (AAP) note that the chance a child will ever need their own stored cord blood is extremely low. They only recommend private storage if an immediate family member already has, or is at high risk of developing, a condition that can be treated with cord blood stem cells.

In the UK, both public and private storage are regulated by the Human Tissue Authority (HTA). Families can donate to the NHS Cord Blood Bank, which operates under strict safety and ethical standards. UK professional guidance also encourages public donation whenever possible.

One practical note: delayed cord clamping — which is beneficial for most babies because it allows extra blood to transfer from the placenta (see above) — can slightly reduce the amount of cord blood available for banking. If you're planning donation or storage, it's a good idea to discuss timing with your care team during pregnancy so you can balance both benefits.

Chapter 6 Checklist:

MINDSET MATTERS

- Fear → tension → pain;
- calm → oxytocin → better flow,
- progress, and comfort.

CONTROL THE CONTROLLABLES

- Prep your tools, team, and environment;
- stay flexible about outcomes.

KNOW THE MAP

- Understanding stages (early/active/transition → pushing → placenta) reduces anxiety.
- better blood flow to uterus.

FUEL EARLY

- Nutritious foods in small portions + steady fluids in pre-/early labour preserve energy for pushing.

When to go to Hospital/Birth Center

- Rule of thumb: 5-1-1 (or 4-1-1 if coping well) and waves getting longer/stronger/closer.

KEEP MOVING

- Different positions, water, massage/counter-pressure, and optional TENS help.

Monitoring choices

- If low-risk, ask for intermittent or wireless monitoring to stay mobile.

PAIN RELIEF SPECTRUM

- Non-drug methods, nitrous/opioids (modest relief),
- epidural (most effective; may lengthen pushing/ raise assisted birth).

PARTNER POWER

- They protect your space, cue breathing/relaxation, advocate, and keep you nourished
- Doula can also complement the team.

DECIDE WITH BRAINS

- Benefits, Risks, Alternatives, Instinct, Nothing (wait), Second opinion.

INDUCTION CLARITY

- Ask *why*, how "ripe" your cervix is, methods planned, and time allowed before "failed."

ASSISTED BIRTH & EPISIOTOMY

- Forceps/vacuum used for specific reasons;
- not a failure—know the why and recovery.

CESAREAN CAN BE CALM

- Discuss music/lighting,
- delayed cord clamping,
- immediate skin-to-skin;

THIRD STAGE CHOICES

- Active vs physiological management,
- delayed cord clamping,
- vitamin K,
- newborn eye ointment—decide ahead of time.

PACK WITH PURPOSE

- Comfort items,
- snacks/fluids,
- birth plan,
- tools so the space feels like *yours*.

BOTTOM LINE

- Preparation + supportive team + adaptable plan = confidence.

POSTPARTUM RECOVERY AND CARE

In this chapter I will mention key factors that affect postpartum health for mothers and families. This is a crucial time when after the euphoria and excitement of bringing your baby into the world a new journey begins and it is at times uplifting, at times challenging and at times can overwhelm.

This is where the support team you have identified can come into their own.

THE FOURTH TRIMESTER: WHAT TO EXPECT POST-DELIVERY

Often known as the 'fourth trimester', this is a delicate yet profound stage that many new parents find transformative and pretty difficult. It is like an extension of pregnancy, where both you and your newborn are still learning and adapting. The concept recognizes that the transition from womb to world isn't instantaneous for your little one. Your baby is adjusting to life outside the womb, learning to breathe, feed, and feel the world around them. Meanwhile, your body is undergoing its own remarkable changes.

In the UK, you might find more structured postpartum support compared to the US. Midwives (days 1-10) and then health visitors (from 11 days to 30 days) make home visits, providing guidance on everything from breastfeeding to emotional well-being, intermittently during the first month of your baby's life. In contrast, postpartum care in the US can feel less coordinated, often requiring more proactive steps from you and your partner to access similar support. It underscores the importance of seeking out help if you are worried or have new symptoms, and building a network around you, through healthcare providers but also in your community. Trust your instincts-if something doesn't feel right, please seek help.

Your body will undergo several physical changes during this time. The uterus starts its journey back to pre-pregnancy size in a process called involution which will take about 6 weeks (also known as the 4th stage). This can lead to lochia discharge—a normal shedding of blood and tissue lasting several weeks. Your breasts will also change, adapting for milk production as your body responds to your baby's needs. It's common to experience some discomfort and mood changes as milk comes in; warm compresses or gentle massages can provide some relief.

Emotionally, this period is a whirlwind. Bonding with your newborn is a beautiful yet complex process. It's normal for emotions to fluctuate as you navigate this new relationship. You might feel immense love and joy, but also moments of doubt or anxiety. The psychological shift into motherhood often brings identity adjustments as you balance your previous self with your new role. These feelings are normal; acknowledging them can help you manage this transition more smoothly.

Rest becomes a pivotal part of recovery, though it might seem elusive with a newborn. Sleep deprivation can exacerbate feelings of overwhelm and affect your mood. Embrace naps whenever possible, aligning rest with your baby's sleep. Even short periods of rest can rejuvenate your mind and body, helping you tackle the challenges of caring for your little one. And don't give up on the relaxing 4/8 breath you learned. This is a lifelong habit that can reset at the most challenging times.

Incorporating quick self-care routines into your day can make a significant difference. A warm shower or a few minutes stroll outside or a little journalling can restore your spirit amidst the demands of motherhood. Remember, self-care isn't selfish; it's essential for maintaining your well-being and capacity to care for your baby.

REFLECTION EXERCISE: REDISCOVERING YOUR IDENTITY

Take a moment each week to reflect on your evolving identity as a mother. Jot down thoughts or feelings that arise during quiet moments in your journal or in the back of this book. Consider what aspects of yourself you wish to nurture alongside motherhood. This exercise can help you stay connected to who you are beyond your role as a parent, offering a sense of continuity while so much in your life is changing.

Supporting each other through this stage is vital for both partners. Sharing responsibilities fosters a sense of teamwork and eases the load on each other. Whether it's taking turns with nighttime feedings or preparing meals together, these actions build a supportive environment where both parents feel valued and cared for.

Building a community around you is equally important. Reaching out to family, friends, or local parent groups can provide both practical help and emotional support. They can offer encouragement, share experiences, and lend a hand when needed. It's okay to ask for help; in fact, it's essential!

PHYSICAL RECOVERY: HEALING AFTER VAGINAL BIRTH

After childbirth, your body's healing process begins, often accompanied by soreness in the perineal area, especially if there was prolonged pushing, tearing or an episiotomy. Expect postpartum bleeding, or lochia, lasting several weeks—a normal cleansing mechanism of shedding the uterine lining. Be observant of clots, which are common but should decrease over time.

Promote recovery and comfort with practical strategies like sitz baths and ice packs for swelling and soreness relief. I remember many hours spent with ice packs in the perineal area, which brought some relief. Although annoying as it is to hear, time was the greatest healer. Pelvic floor exercises, like Kegels, are simple yet effective in muscle recovery and can be done anywhere. Allow your body sufficient time to heal and please be gentle with yourself.

A sitz bath is a warm, shallow soak for the perineal area (the space between the vulva/vagina and the anus). IUse it to soothe pain, swelling, and itching, improve blood flow, and promote healing. Commonly after birth you may be healing from, episiotomy/tears, hemorrhoids, or anal fissures.

- Use a clean sitz-bath basin that fits on the toilet *or* a very clean bathtub.

- Fill with **warm** water

- Soak 10–15 minutes, 1–3 times/day. Plain water is best; some people add a little **Epsom salts** if not irritating.

- Pat dry gently (don't rub); a cool pack after can help.

When to be cautious/avoid:

- If there are any signs of infection (fever, foul-smelling discharge, worsening redness), **heavy bleeding**, or if your clinician advised against soaking.

- Avoid perfumed soaps/oils that can irritate.

- If you have stitches, sitz baths are generally fine—just keep the water clean and follow your provider's guidance.

While most postpartum symptoms are normal, watch for signs indicating complications—excessive bleeding, large clots, infection signs such as fever or foul-smelling discharge warrant immediate healthcare consultation. Trust your instincts and seek medical advice if needed. It is also normal to feel tired, if not exhausted, in the postpartum period but even that may need checking out if excessive. My friend was diagnosed with thyroiditis in the postpartum period, which causes excessive exhaustion due to reduced thyroid hormone production, for which she needed to take replacement, so please reach out, your symptoms may need further investigation.

Resuming intimacy varies; typically, some healthcare providers suggest waiting four to six weeks before intercourse to ensure proper healing but this is up to you. You will know when you feel ready. But don't forget to discuss contraception options with your healthcare provider to find what suits you best. Remember, if you are breastfeeding you will not likely have your monthly period.

EMOTIONAL WELLNESS: MANAGING POSTPARTUM MOOD CHANGES

Post-birth emotions can be unpredictable, ranging from the common "baby blues" to more serious conditions like postpartum depression or anxiety. Baby blues—mood swings, weepiness, and exhaustion—usually appear in the first days after delivery, particularly marked when your milk comes in, and can resolve within a couple of weeks. If these feelings persist or intensify, it may signal postpartum depression, which is a medical condition that needs professional care. Anxiety is also common, reflecting the new responsibilities of caring for a newborn. Recognizing these experiences as part of postpartum adjustment is crucial—you are not alone.

Daily routines and mindfulness can provide stability. Simple rituals like a morning walk, coffee, or quiet time with your baby act as grounding anchors. Even brief mindfulness practices, such as the relaxing breath or meditation, can reduce stress and increase calm.

Support is vital. I cannot emphasize this enough. Partners and family/friends play an essential role—listening without judgment, encouraging open communication, and making space for self-care all help create a nurturing environment for recovery. Talking with a therapist offers a safe space to process emotions and learn coping strategies, while support groups connect you with others experiencing similar challenges.

BREASTFEEDING BASICS: GETTING STARTED WITH CONFIDENCE

Breastfeeding provides unmatched benefits for both mother and baby. Breast milk is rich in nutrients and antibodies that boost your baby's immune system, protect against illness, and support growth. For mothers, breastfeeding aids postpartum recovery, lowers the risk of certain cancers, and deepens the bond through skin-to-skin connection.

Getting started takes practice. A proper latch is key for effective feeding and to prevent soreness. Hold your baby tummy-to-tummy, align their nose with your nipple, and wait for a wide mouth before guiding them on. It is important to know that breastfeeding is NOT nipple feeding. It is called breastfeeding because the latch needs to include more of the breast tissue than just the nipple so that the baby is really able to compress the milk ducts and get milk effectively. This will also be more comfortable for you and should cause less nipple soreness. Honestly, if the latch is painful it is not correct. Take baby off by slipping your little finger between their mouth and your breast and break the suction. Then try again, and have baby latch when their mouth is widest open so they can get a good amount of breast tissue in their mouth. Experiment with positions like cradle, cross-cradle, or football hold to find comfort. Allow your baby to finish on one breast before switching to ensure they get both foremilk (for thirst) and hind milk (for growth). Watch for early hunger cues—rooting, sucking motions, or hand-to-mouth movements—to avoid frantic feeds.

Challenges are honestly quite common but recognizing these early will help with management. Engorgement can be eased by expressing a little milk before feeding, using warm compresses beforehand, and cool compresses afterward. Flat nipples may benefit from a pump or nipple shield. I had huge problems with getting a good latch with my first due to flat nipples. Each pregnancy got slightly better but the hand expressing for me, before feeding, was our only chance for a decent latch at least in the beginning before my milk supply settled. To support milk supply, nurse frequently, stay hydrated, and eat well. I understand this is sometimes easier said than done.

I know I keep talking about support, but honestly this period, almost more than any other around having a baby, it is crucial. Lactation consultants provide tailored guidance, and support groups or family encouragement can offer reassurance and techniques. If breastfeeding doesn't go as planned, pumping or formula can be healthy alternatives—what matters most is that your baby thrives and you feel supported.

With my first, I had to mix feed by 28 days and as a health professional I felt quite the failure. The hospital I lived close to were so helpful and I even had milk from their bank while I was trying to build up my supply. In retrospect I probably should have mixed sooner. He was losing weight and not thriving, but it is hard to see these things with the mix of emotions and exhaustion all playing a part in clouding my judgement. And why, are we, as mothers, so hard on ourselves? This is the most difficult, rewarding, joyous journey you can take. We must allow ourselves grace.

PARTNER SUPPORT POSTPARTUM: CARING FOR EACH OTHER

The postpartum period is a major transition for both parents, and partner support is vital. I've already mentioned sharing responsibilities like nighttime feedings, diaper changes, meal prep, and chores. Emotional reassurance matters as much as practical help. Listening without judgment, offering empathy, and providing small gestures of affection create a safe space for vulnerability and connection. This environment allows both partners to adapt to new roles with trust and cooperation.

Amidst newborn care, it's important to nurture the relationship itself. Simple rituals—watching a movie together, enjoying a walk, or having an at-home date night—help maintain intimacy and balance. Encouraging each other to take breaks for rest or personal hobbies preserves individual well-being and sustains resilience.

Open, honest communication underpins everything. Sharing concerns, celebrating small milestones, and supporting each other's needs foster mutual understanding and stability. By caring for one another as well as your baby, you build a strong, unified foundation for family life.

BUILDING YOUR VILLAGE: CREATING A SUPPORTIVE COMMUNITY

A strong support network is a lifeline during the postpartum period. Emotional validation from others reminds you that you're not alone, while practical help—like meals, errands, or childcare—creates space for rest, recovery, and bonding with your baby. Reaching out isn't weakness; it's self-care.

If your budget allows, in those early few weeks you can consider a postpartum doula. They can help support your breastfeeding schedule, help prepare nourishing meals, and support you as you support your baby.

Community resources can expand your circle. Local parent groups, meetups, provide camaraderie, shared experiences, and advice from people who truly understand. These connections can reduce isolation, offer new perspectives, and even grow into lasting friendships. I cannot emphasize enough the peer support of meeting with other mothers. The women I was paired with in my childbirth classes all those years ago, remain close friends today. The support I received from them, especially during my intense breastfeeding difficulties, was invaluable. And the mutual support we could offer each other through the emotional ups and downs of the first few weeks, and then years, has been such a special part of my life.

If family and friends are nearby they can also play a pivotal role. Regular visits or check-ins provide comfort and tangible support, from helping around the house to giving you breaks for self-care. Clear boundaries are essential—communicating your needs and preferences ensures support feels helpful rather than overwhelming. Accepting assistance graciously strengthens bonds and lightens your load.

Ultimately, your "village" is about surrounding yourself with people who lift you up, provide stability, and celebrate your wins. With this foundation, you can move through postpartum challenges with greater confidence and connection.

One day I hope to write a book to accompany this one that concentrates solely on the postpartum period. It is not a stage to take lightly and the adaptation to family life can be challenging. It is never quite what you expect and emotions can be conflicting. I hope that you are able to find support that speaks to you. I have added some essential phone numbers in the resources section in case you find yourself in need. Don't hesitate to call if you need it.

Chapter 7 Checklist:

THE FOURTH TRIMESTER IS REAL

- This 6–12 week transition is an extension of pregnancy — a time of healing, adaptation, and emotional transformation for both mother and baby.

YOUR SUPPORT NETWORK MATTERS

- Identify and lean on your "village" — partner, doula, family, friends,
- midwife, or health visitor — for emotional, physical, and practical help.

KNOW WHAT'S NORMAL

- Uterine involution, lochia, breast engorgement,
- mood fluctuations are expected;
- seek help for fever, heavy bleeding, or persistent distress.

REST AND RECOVERY ARE VITAL

- If you can, sleep when baby sleeps, hydrate,
- use your 4/8 breath to reset — even brief pauses help your mind and body recover.

SELF-CARE IS NOT SELFISH

- Small rituals — a warm shower, short walk, journaling, or quiet tea — can anchor you amid the demands of early motherhood.

REFLECT ON YOUR IDENTITY

- Journal weekly about your evolving self — motherhood adds layers, not replacements, to who you are.

PARTNERS PLAY A CRUCIAL ROLE

- Share duties, communicate openly, and nurture your relationship to maintain connection and teamwork.

PHYSICAL RECOVERY TAKES TIME

- Sitz baths, ice packs, gentle movement,
- pelvic-floor exercises ease soreness and speed healing.

WATCH FOR WARNING SIGNS

- Heavy bleeding, foul discharge, fever, or worsening pain warrant prompt medical attention.

EMOTIONAL WELLBEING FLUCTUATES

- "Baby blues" are common;
- persistent sadness or anxiety needs professional help.
- You are not alone.

BREASTFEEDING IS A LEARNED SKILL

- A deep latch prevents soreness and supports milk flow;
- lactation consultants and peer groups are invaluable.

FEEDING IS ABOUT NOURISHMENT

- Whether breast, bottle, or mixed — what matters most is that baby thrives and you feel supported.

BUILD YOUR VILLAGE

- Join local parent groups, postpartum circles, or online communities — shared experiences ease isolation and boost confidence.
- Set boundaries and accept help.
- Allow others to assist with meals, chores, or rest breaks; communicate your needs clearly.

GRACE ABOVE ALL

- Parenthood is beautiful and messy.
- Be gentle with yourself — healing takes time.

CONCLUSION

Pregnancy and Birth Made Calm: The Evidence-Based Guide to a Safe, Healthy Pregnancy and a Positive Birth Experience was written to offer information with clarity that calms you. My aim has been simple and consistent: use good evidence, plain language, enable you with knowledge and practical skills so you can navigate this experience with calm at the center.

Throughout the book, I have returned to the same core idea: calm is not a personality trait; it is something you can learn, practice and take with you when you deliver your baby and will give you a lifelong way to steady yourself every day. You learned what is likely to happen in each trimester, how to look after yourself, and how to prepare your body and mind for labor. Evidence provided a framework; your values and circumstances are at the core of this experience for you and your family..

As birth approaches, keep your anchors in view. Choose the place and team you trust. Ask good questions—about benefits, risks, and alternatives for you and your baby right now—and give yourself permission to pause long enough to think. Hold preferences for unmedicated labor, for epidural support, and for cesarean, not because you expect to use all three, but because readiness reduces anxiety and expands your options. Plans can change; your preparation and priorities do not.

During labor, remember that calm is practical. Have your toolkit list handy. Use the breathing patterns I have taught to help you settle. Shift your position to invite progress. Use water, heat, music, rhythm and touch whenever they help. Adjust lighting and sound to protect your attention. Keep communication quiet, simple and specific. Invite your partner or support person to take real roles—timing contractions, offering counter-pressure, asking clarifying questions, and guarding your space so you can focus on the work only you can do.

If decisions arise quickly, lean on the tools you have rehearsed. Name what matters most to you, ask what the care team is most concerned about, and decide the next right step with the information you have. Birth is unpredictable; feeling unprepared is optional. You have a map, and you have practiced how to move when the path shifts.

After birth, apply the same steady approach to the early days at home. Protect rest and recovery. Feed your body well and often. Watch your bleeding, pain, mood, and pelvic floor, and ask for help and support early. Accept that learning your baby will take time. A small set of routines—skin-to-skin, responsive feeding, outdoor walks, short check-ins with your support network—will do more for your wellbeing than any complicated plan.

No one does this alone. Build and use your circle—partner, family, doulas, lactation specialists, pelvic health physiotherapists, perinatal mental-health resources, and trusted peers. Share what you have learned here with them so everyone is working from the same page. Calm is easier to sustain when your environment helps you hold onto it.

If your birth story looks different from what you had first imagined, know that difference does not cancel out a positive experience. Safety and health come first; agency and compassion shape how the day is remembered. Your preparation, your voice, and the care you received still belong to your story. Make sure to have time to debrief about your experience with your support network.

This guide cannot promise a particular outcome and is also not exhaustive. Conditions can arise that are not included in the scope of this book. But in those circumstances, lean into trusted health care professionals.

What this book can do is promise a way of approaching pregnancy and birth that respects you as the decision-maker and equips you with knowledge as a tool that works.

May what you've learned here help you meet labor with steadiness, welcome your baby with confidence, and step into the early weeks with a clear sense of what matters most to your family.

You are ready.

Know Your Body

Trust Your Body

Own Your Birth.

REFERENCES

CHAPTER 1/2:

Safety of 'flu shot in pregnancy:
https://pmc.ncbi.nlm.nih.gov/articles/PMC6605784/

Safety of TDaP in pregnancy:
https://www.ncbi.nlm.nih.gov/books/NBK582551/

Safety of mRNA COVID19 vaccine in pregnancy:
https://pmc.ncbi.nlm.nih.gov/articles/PMC10040368/

RSV vaccination in pregnancy:
https://pubmed.ncbi.nlm.nih.gov/38695784/

Steps to a Healthier me and baby-to-be! checklist
https://www.cdc.gov/pregnancy/media/pdfs/Pregnancy_Planner_508.
pdf

Effects of lifestyle factors on fertility
https://pmc.ncbi.nlm.nih.gov/articles/
PMC8812443/#:~:text=Several%20authors%20have%20provided%20
evidence,caffeine%20consumption%2C%20exercise%2C%20risky%20
sexual

Fertility https://pmc.ncbi.nlm.nih.gov/articles/PMC188498/

Prenatal vitamins: Why they matter, how to choose
https://www.mayoclinic.org/healthy-lifestyle/pregnancy-week-by-week/in-depth/prenatal-vitamins/art-20046945#:~:text=Beyond%20checking%20for%20folic%20acid,B%20vitamins%2C%20zinc%20and%20iodine.

The menstrual cycle:
https://www.betterhealth.vic.gov.au/health/conditionsandtreatments/menstrual-cycle

Symptoms of pregnancy: What happens first
https://www.mayoclinic.org/healthy-lifestyle/getting-pregnant/in-depth/symptoms-of-pregnancy/art-20043853

Morning sickness - Diagnosis and treatment - Mayo Clinic
https://www.mayoclinic.org/diseases-conditions/morning-sickness/diagnosis-treatment/drc-20375260

Pregnancy diet: Focus on these essential nutrients
https://www.mayoclinic.org/healthy-lifestyle/pregnancy-week-by-week/in-depth/pregnancy-nutrition/art-20045082

Caffeine intake:
https://www.acog.org/womens-health/experts-and-stories/ask-acog/how-much-coffee-can-i-drink-while-pregnant

Emotional Changes in Pregnancy
https://www.tommys.org/pregnancy-information/im-pregnant/mental-wellbeing/emotional-changes-pregnancy

CHAPTER 3:

Fetal development: The second trimester
https://www.mayoclinic.org/healthy-lifestyle/pregnancy-week-by-week/in-depth/fetal-development/art-20046151

Eating Well in Your Second Trimester
https://www.healthline.com/health/pregnancy/
second-trimester-diet-nutrition

Self-Care During Pregnancy - Women's Health Issues
https://www.merckmanuals.com/home/women-s-health-issues/
normal-pregnancy/self-care-during-pregnancy

The role of the partner in the support of a pregnant woman's
healthy diet https://bmcpregnancychildbirth.biomedcentral.com/
articles/10.1186/s12884-023-06072-9

Maternal outcomes in pregnancy
https://www.sciencedirect.com/science/article/pii/
S0168851024001647

Maternal Outcomes in those who Planned home births
https://www.thelancet.com/journals/eclinm/article/
PIIS2589-5370(20)30063-8/fulltext

US Maternal Mortality
https://www.bmj.com/content/385/bmj.q1276#:~:text=In%20
2022%2C%2022%20US%20women,were%20preventable%2C%20
the%20report%20says.

Planned home births
https://pmc.ncbi.nlm.nih.gov/articles/PMC11542973/

CHAPTER 4:

Grantly Dick-Reed "Childbirth Without Fear" Available from
Amazon re-issue published in 2013

What Is Hypnobirthing? Technique, How-To, Pros and Cons
https://www.healthline.com/health/pregnancy/hypnobirthing

Benefits of HypnoBirthing | What Expecting Parents Gain
https://hypnobirthing.com/benefits/

Women's experiences with hypnobirth – A qualitative study
https://www.sciencedirect.com/science/article/pii/
S1877575623000800

Positive Birth Stories | Stories of Calm, Peaceful HypnoBirths
https://hypnobirthing.com/birth-stories/

Anatomy Autonomic Nervous System
https://www.ncbi.nlm.nih.gov/books/NBK539845/#:~:text=The%20
autonomic%20nervous%20system%20is,sympathetic%2C%20
parasympathetic%2C%20and%20enteric.

Unconscious or subconscious
https://www.health.harvard.edu/blog/
unconscious-or-subconscious-20100801255

CHAPTER 5:

Your third trimester pregnancy guide and checklist - BabyCenter
https://www.babycenter.com/pregnancy/your-body/
the-ultimate-pregnancy-to-do-list-third-trimester_10341209

The accuracy of ultrasound estimation of fetal weight
https://pmc.ncbi.nlm.nih.gov/articles/PMC5810856/

The Effect of Doulas on Maternal and Birth Outcomes
https://pmc.ncbi.nlm.nih.gov/articles/PMC10292163/

3rd trimester pregnancy: What to expect
https://www.mayoclinic.org/healthy-lifestyle/
pregnancy-week-by-week/in-depth/pregnancy/art-20046767

Pack your bag for labour
https://www.nhs.uk/pregnancy/labour-and-birth/
preparing-for-the-birth/pack-your-bag-for-labour/

Birthing Center vs Hospital: What Are the Differences
https://nursingcecentral.com/
birthing-center-vs-hospital-what-are-the-differences/

Tokophobia (Fear of Childbirth)
https://my.clevelandclinic.org/health/
diseases/22711-tokophobia-fear-of-childbirth

Sample birth plan ACOG
https://www.acog.org/-/media/project/acog/
acogorg/womens-health/files/ health-tools/sample-
birth-plan. pdf?rev=0fa1905fa89d4be3b852348
4d4aaa386&hash=041EB0E392B7FEE88 0257A3FAE6E6565

NHS Birth plan
https://www.nhs.uk/pregnancy/labour-and-birth/
preparing-for-the-birth/how-to-make-a-birth-plan/

CHAPTER 6

Consuming Dates in late pregnancy to help with labor outcomes
https://pubmed.ncbi.nlm.nih.gov/21280989/

Raspberry leaf tea in late pregnancy
https://pmc.ncbi.nlm.nih.gov/articles/PMC7871383/

Evening Primrose Oil in late pregnancy
https://pmc.ncbi.nlm.nih.gov/articles/PMC9947258/

Normal Labor: Physiology, Evaluation, and Management
https://www.ncbi.nlm.nih.gov/books/NBK544290/

Support During Labor and Childbirth
https://www.ncbi.nlm.nih.gov/books/NBK304186/

Perineal Massage

Beckmann, M. M., & Garrett, A. J. (2017). *Antenatal perineal massage for reducing perineal trauma.* **Cochrane Database of Systematic Reviews,** Issue 4. doi:10.1002/14651858.CD005123.pub3

Perineal Massage

National Institute for Health and Care Excellence (NICE). *Intrapartum care for healthy women and babies (NG235),* 2023.

ACOG Committee Opinion No. 736: *Optimizing Support for Vaginal Birth,* 2018.

Membrane sweeping for induction of labor
https://pmc.ncbi.nlm.nih.gov/articles/PMC7044809/

Continuous Fetal Monitoring in Labor
https://pubmed.ncbi.nlm.nih.gov/38754249/

Medically Indicated Late Preterm and Early Term Deliveries
https://www.acog.org/clinical/clinical-guidance/committee-opinion/articles/2021/07/medically-indicated-late-preterm-and-early-term-deliveries?utm_source

Labor Induction vs Expectant Management (ARRIVE study)
https://starlegacyfoundation.org/wp-content/uploads/Grobman-2018-Labor-Induction-vs-Expectant-Management-ARRIVE.pdf

Critique of ARRIVE study
https://pmc.ncbi.nlm.nih.gov/articles/PMC6821557/#:~:text=Selection%20bias%20is%20a%20concern,but%20not%20in%20the%20study.

Epidurals for Pain relief in labor-Cochrane review
https://www.cochrane.org/evidence/CD000331_epidurals-pain-relief-labour?utm_source

Epidural versus non-epidural or no analgesia for pain relief in labor
https://pmc.ncbi.nlm.nih.gov/articles/PMC6494646/?utm_source

Medications for Pain Relief During Labor and Delivery
https://www.acog.org/womens-health/faqs/
medications-for-pain-relief-during-labor-and-delivery?utm_source

Recommendations for Intrapartum Care NICE Guidelines (UK)
https://www.nice.org.uk/guidance/ng235/chapter/
Recommendations?utm_source

Pain Relief in Labor and Birth
https://www.nhs.uk/pregnancy/labour-and-birth/what-happens/
pain-relief-in-labour/?utm_source

Use of Nitrous Oxide in Labor
https://www.acog.org/clinical/clinical-guidance/practice-advisory/
articles/2021/07/use-of-nitrous-oxide-in-labor-and-possible-
interaction-with-systemic-opioids-or-sedatives-hypnotics?utm_
source

Vaginal Breech Delivery
https://pmc.ncbi.nlm.nih.gov/articles/PMC10309230/
https://pmc.ncbi.nlm.nih.gov/articles/PMC9284475/

The Risk Of Cesarean Delivery with Neuraxial Analgesia Given Early
Versus Late in Labor
https://www.nejm.org/doi/full/10.1056/NEJMoa042573?utm_source

Modern Labor Epidural Analgesia
https://www.sciencedirect.com/science/article/pii/
S000293782200463X?utm_source

WHO recommendations for the prevention and treatment of
postpartum haemorrhage. Geneva: World Health Organization.
https://apps.who.int/iris/handle/10665/75411

Active versus expectant management for women in the third stage of labour. https://doi.org/10.1002/14651858.CD007412.pub5

Royal College of Obstetricians and Gynaecologists (RCOG). (2016). *Preventing maternal deaths caused by postpartum haemorrhage.* Green-top Guideline No. 52. London: RCOG.

American College of Obstetricians and Gynecologists (ACOG). (2017). *Practice Bulletin No. 183: Postpartum hemorrhage.* Obstetrics & Gynecology, 130(4), e168–e186. https://doi.org/10.1097/AOG.0000000000002351

Evidence-based labor management-3rd Stage https://pubmed.ncbi.nlm.nih.gov/35537683/

Delayed Cord Clamping Delayed Umbilical Cord Clamping After Birth | ACOG

Vitamin K and the newborn Infant https://journals.lww.com/greenjournal/fulltext/2025/09000/acog_clinical_practice_update__an_update_to.22.aspx?utm_source

Prophylactic Vitamin K https://pubmed.ncbi.nlm.nih.gov/11034761/

Inducing Labour NICE Guidelines (UK) https://www.nice.org.uk/guidance/ng207/resources/inducing-labour-pdf-66143719773637

Induction of Labor at or after 37 weeks gestation https://pubmed.ncbi.nlm.nih.gov/32666584/

Randomized Trial of Labor Induction in Women 35 Year or Older https://www.nejm.org/doi/full/10.1056/NEJMoa1509117?utm_source

Trial of Labor After Cesarean https://www.sciencedirect.com/science/article/abs/pii/S1701216318309034?utm_source

Cervical Ripening in the Outpatient Setting
https://effectivehealthcare.ahrq.gov/sites/default/files/cer-238-
cervical-ripening-evidence-summary.pdf?utm_source

Labor Induction ACOG
https://www.acog.org/womens-health/faqs/labor-induction?utm_
source=chatgpt.com

First and Second Stage Labor Management
https://www.acog.org/clinical/clinical-guidance/
clinical-practice-guideline/articles/2024/01/
first-and-second-stage-labor-management?utm_source

The Role of Oxytocin and the Effect of Stress during Childhood
https://pubmed.ncbi.nlm.nih.gov/34777247/

Oxytocin and the Development of Parenting in Humans
https://pmc.ncbi.nlm.nih.gov/articles/PMC3943240/?utm_source

Mother-Infant Skin to Skin Contact: Short- and Long-Term Effects
for Mothers
https://pmc.ncbi.nlm.nih.gov/articles/PMC7485314/?utm_source

Oxytocin and the Microbiome
https://www.sciencedirect.com/science/article/pii/
S2666497623000395?utm_sourcem

Natural Childbirth Linked to Stronger Baby Bonding than C-sections
https://medicine.yale.edu/news-article/natural-childbirth-linked-to-
stronger-baby-bonding-than-c-sections/?utm_source

Assisted Vaginal Birth
https://www.rcog.org.uk/guidance/
browse-all-guidance/green-top-guidelines/
assisted-vaginal-birth-green-top-guideline-no-26/?utm_source

Instruments for Assisted Vaginal Birth
https://www.cochrane.org/evidence/CD005455_instruments-assisted-vaginal-birth?utm_source=chatgpt.com

Vacuum Assisted Vaginal Delivery
https://pmc.ncbi.nlm.nih.gov/articles/PMC2672989/?utm_source

Recommendations Cesarean Birth NICE Guidelines
https://www.nice.org.uk/guidance/ng192/chapter/recommendations?utm_source

Risks of Cesarean Section (NHS)
https://www.nhs.uk/tests-and-treatments/caesarean-section/risks/

Tita ATN et al. "Adjunctive Azithromycin Prophylaxis for Cesarean Delivery." *New England Journal of Medicine.*2016;375:1231–1241.

ACOG Practice Bulletin No. 205: Vaginal Birth After Cesarean Delivery. Obstet Gynecol. 2019;133:e110–e127.

Lippincott Obstetrics & Gynecology Review, 2022.

Episiotomy Use Among Vaginal Deliveries and the Association with Anal Sphincter Injury
https://pmc.ncbi.nlm.nih.gov/articles/PMC6805174/?utm_source

Why Giving Birth is Safer in the UK than the US
https://www.propublica.org/article/why-giving-birth-is-safer-in-britain-than-in-the-u-s#:~:text=The%20numbers%20reflect%20the%20difference,recognized%20and%20managed%20in%20time.

Evidence-Based Labor Management-3rd Stage
https://pubmed.ncbi.nlm.nih.gov/35537683/

Maternal Outcomes and Birth Interventions in Women Who Begin Labor Intending to Give Birth at Home
https://www.thelancet.com/journals/eclinm/article/PIIS2589-5370(20)30063-8/fulltext#:~:text=After%20accounting%20for%20

parity%2C%20women,interventions%20and%20untoward%20
birth%20outcomes.

Quality Improvement Strategies for Safe Reduction of Primary
Cesarean Births
https://www.acog.org/clinical/clinical-guidance/committee-
statement/articles/2025/04/quality-improvement-strategies-for-safe-
reduction-of-primary-cesarean-birth?utm_source

Fast Stats- Births- Method of Delivery
https://www.cdc.gov/nchs/fastats/delivery.htm?utm_source

New England Journal of Medicine (C-SOAP trial, 2016).

CHAPTER 7

What Postpartum Care Looks Like Around the World,
https://www.healthline.com/health/pregnancy/what-post-childbirth-
care-looks-like-around-the-world-and-why-the-u-s-is-missing-the-
mark

Postpartum depression - Symptoms and causes
https://www.mayoclinic.org/diseases-conditions/
postpartum-depression/symptoms-causes/syc-20376617

Breastfeeding Techniques: 10 Effective Practices to Try
https://www.healthline.com/health/breastfeeding/
breastfeeding-techniques

How to be a Supportive Postpartum Partner
https://boramcare.com/
how-to-be-a-supportive-partner-during-postpartum/

Essential Newborn Care: A Guide for First-Time Parents
https://commonwealthpeds.com/
essential-newborn-care-first-time-parents/

Safe Sleep https://www.aap.org/en/patient-care/safe-sleep/?srsltid=AfmBOoqLOvdlwN_cG8XSo1Sot49-yKEL30iE-zBC6p457K8FNY5dms0b

Breastfeeding vs. Formula Feeding Information https://www.mountsinai.org/health-library/special-topic/breastfeeding-vs-formula-feeding

Bonding and attachment: newborns https://raisingchildren.net.au/newborns/connecting-communicating/bonding/bonding-newborns

Identity Shift In Motherhood - Council for Relationships https://councilforrelationships.org/identity-shift-in-motherhood-navigating-new-challenges-rediscovering-yourself/#:~:text=Embarking%20on%20the%20journey%20of,amidst%20the%20chaos%20of%20parenting.

23 Effective Time Management Strategies for Moms https://organizedchaosblog.com/time-management-for-moms/

Nurturing Intimacy: A Guide to Sex and Connection After Birth https://www.postpartum.net/nurturing-intimacy-a-guide-to-sex-and-connection-after-childbirth/#:~:text=Engaging%20in%20activities%20that%20promote,%2C%20understanding%2C%20and%20open%20communication.

Exercise after pregnancy: How to get started https://www.mayoclinic.org/healthy-lifestyle/labor-and-delivery/in-depth/exercise-after-pregnancy/art-20044596

General Notes

General Notes

General Notes

General Notes

Birth Plan Notes

Think about including:

Birth environment including lighting/sounds/quiet

Terminology you want used

Companions for birth

Birthing Equipment you want to use

Special facilities like tubs

Examinations

Monitoring

Keeping Active

Positions for labor and birth

Pain relief options

Induction

Episiotomy

Instrumental Delivery

Surgical Birth (Cesarean)

Skin to skin contact

Delayed cord clamping

Placenta delivery

Vitamin K

Eye drops

Feeding my baby

Special requirements like interpretation/cultural/religious etc

Any further notes

____
____
____
____
____
____
____
____
____
____
____
____
____
____
____

Birth Plan Notes contd.

Hospital Bag checklist

FOR YOU:

- Comfortable clothes for early labor
- Change of clothes
- Going home outfit
- Nightshirt-button down best
- Robe
- Comfy socks
- Non-slip slippers
- Hair ties or scrunchy for long hair and hairbrush
- Nursing bra/tank
- Breast pads
- Button down nightshirt for after birth
- (Throwaway) large underwear
- Large pads (maxi)
- Toiletries including toothbrush, toothpaste, deodorant, body lotion/ oil, shampoo, face wipes, possibly body wipes
- Snacks/smoothies in cooler
- Water bottle
- Phone and charger
- Documents-ID/ insurance card/ important phone numbers list/birth plan/ list of affirmations
- Wallet
- Birthing or peanut Ball
- Your own pillow
- Your own blanket
- Tennis/lacrosse ball for massage
- Camera
- TENS machine (possibly from Doula)

FOR YOUR PARTNER:

- Change of clothes
- Toiletries
- Snacks
- Water Bottle
- Electronics plus charger

FOR THE ROOM:

- Portable speaker
- tealights/other items for atmosphere
- Blanket from home
- Anchor
- Diffuser
- Extra batteries

FOR BABY:

- Car seat
- Going home outfit-2
- Blanket
- Hat
- Newborn Diapers
- Wipes

Labor Toolkit Ideas-add your own personal ones

- Music playlists

- Positions chart-write down which you think you will like best-remember hands and knees for back pain

- Gentle Physical Affection-hugging, kissing, holding hands, cuddling

- Positive affirmations written down

- Meditations to play

- Visualisations to play

- Massage/massage oil-write down favorites you have practiced

- Picture of box for box breathing visual

- Birthing Comb

- Birthing Ball

- Rhythm

- Aromatherapy-bring diffuser with extra batteries

- Rock/sway

- Dim lights/soft blanket

- TENS unit

Labor Positions

-think about changing positions every 30 minutes. Rhythmic movement within these positions is generally helpful, so you are never static. Practice these BEFORE LABOR, with your partner, so you know which ones seem good for you. Add to your toolkit.

STANDING-all help move baby down with gravity

- with one foot up on chair
- leaning forward with hands on back of chair
- standing with partner behind you
- standing with hands at your back, wide stance (gentle swaying can help)

KNEELING-can relieve back pain and help optimize baby's position

- on all fours
- kneeling with head up on front of chair
- on knees with head resting on a pillow so bottom higher than head

SITTING-allows gravity to help baby descend and good for resting in between contractions

- on birthing ball with partner in front of you so you can lean forward onto them
- in rocking chair

- sitting on a chair facing the back, so you can rest your head on back of chair
- semi-reclined on pillows
- sitting on chair with partner behind
- sitting cross legged

SQUATTING-uses gravity and widens pelvis

- squatting facing your partner for support/ grabbing a bar or something firm in front of you
- squatting with partner kneeling behind you
- squatting with partner standing behind you

The next page shows some visuals to add into the mix. Remember to practice these before labor and write your favorites on your toolkit list.

Your Birth Experience Debrief

Important Resources

PERINATAL MENTAL HEALTH:

Postpartum Support International
https://postpartum.net/

Maternal Mental Health Resource Alliance
https://www.mmhla.org/

Maternal Mental Health Now
https://maternalmentalhealthnow.org/

LACTATION SUPPORT:

IBCLC directories: USLCA Find an IBCLC
(International Board Certified Lactation Consultant)
https://lactationnetwork.com/blog/what-is-an-ibclc/

Peer support: La Leche League
https://llli.org/

Clinical guidance: Academy of Breastfeeding Medicine
(ABM) Protocols (professional but parent-useful)
https://www.bfmed.org/

Medication & milk safety: LactMed (NIH database)
You can look up medications that are passed through to
breast milk
https://www.ncbi.nlm.nih.gov/books/NBK501922/

PELVIC FLOOR PT

APTA Pelvic Health

https://www.aptapelvichealth.org/ "Find a PT"

BIRTH DOULAS AND POSTPARTUM DOULAS:

www.bornbir.com

www.doulamatch.com

CPR TRAINING CLASSES

www.redcross.org

www.ingramcontent.com/pod-product-compliance
Lightning Source LLC
Chambersburg PA
CBHW071456140726
47997CB00005B/1750